MW00716886

RHEATOWN
TENNESSEE

first settled in 1771

The Overmountain Press
JOHNSON CITY, TENNESSEE

ACKNOWLEDGEMENTS

A special thank you to J. Allen Bolinger for his many hours drawing the sketches, writing captions, and assembling the material for the printer.

Affectionate tribute to Jeannie Laws Luttrell for her patience and many hours spent in proofreading the manuscript.

To Mrs. John (Mary Martha Phillips) Hite for suggestions to improve the manuscript, we are deeply grateful.

A thank you to our typists, Pauline D. Monk and Peggy Balding, who worked on the book from its inception to the final rough draft.

Gratitude to Nova Tranbarger who showed professional skill and tireless dedication in typing the final manuscript.

SOURCES OF INFORMATION

Tennessee Annals; Zella Armstrong, historian; Capt. J.J. Marshall's Scrapbook, (furnished by his daughters, Dorothy Marshall and Thelma Marshall Campbell); William Flavorian Piper, newspaperman and teacher; Harry Roberts; **Goodspeed, History of Tennessee, 1887**; Clay Middleton, **Recollections of Rheatown**; Carl N. Hayes, "**Neighbor Against Neighbor**"; *History of Greene County*, 1950, Martha Thomas Chambers; D.D. Alexander's last article to **Greeneville Sun** (Submitted by Kathleen Cannon Mysinger); Judge S.C. Williams, historian; First Register of Rheatown Methodist Church South, 1871-1909, submitted by Robert R. Broyles; Methodist Church 1844, submitted by Ray Maupin; Richard Doughty, **Greeneville - One Hundred Year Portrait - 1775-1875**; Josephine Divine, Randall Moody, Irene Keebler Rowe, Keene White and Joseph Maupin.

(Above credits as listed in original printing in 1977)

First printed in 1977
Revised and reprinted in 1986
ISBN 0-932807-18-6
Copyright © 1986 by The Overmountain Press
All Rights Reserved
Printed in the United States of America

HELEN THOMAS McCURRY
December 9, 1909 - May 25, 1981

The third edition of the book **Rheatown** is dedicated to Helen Thomas McCurry, who was the prime promoter in its first publication in 1977.

Born Helen Madaline Thomas on December 9, 1909, in the little village of Rheatown, she was the third child of William Earle and Lulu White Thomas. The family moved to Jonesborough and later to Chattanooga in her early childhood, but returned to Rheatown while she was still in elementary school. She graduated from Chuckey High School in 1927 and attended East Tennessee State Normal School before starting a teaching career in Greene County. An excellent bookkeeper and cashier, she was employed at H.T. Hackney Co. in Greeneville and at Security Feed and Seed Co. in Johnson City. She managed the Chuckey High School cafeteria and later worked at Barlow's Market and Jaynes Market in Limestone.

On June 15, 1930, she married O.L. (Jack) McCurry, who also lived near Rheatown. They built their home, *Idlewood*, on the McCurry property which they farmed until 1950 when they formed the McCurry Insurance Agency.

Helen joined the Rheatown Methodist Church in 1940. She served on the official board, was a Sunday School teacher for the teens, and was church pianist. She served as church treasurer for several years. As a member of the United Methodist Women, she had served in every office at some point in time and always attended District meetings and Conference meetings.

She was instrumental in getting the Rheatown Cemetery Association formed and was maintenance treasurer. She was a charter member of the Chuckey Home Demonstration and had served as its president. She was also a member of the Greene County Retired Teachers Association and the Greater Limestone Parish Mature Years, serving as its secretary.

Helen had a simple faith and a deep love and concern which touched the lives of everyone who knew her. The ideals of Christian faith were her philosophy for life. She believed in the dignity of work and helping others, doing every job well and always giving more than was expected of her. She was happiest when entertaining her family and friends in her lovely country home, which was surrounded by the many flowers she enjoyed growing.

Helen saw one of her greatest dreams come true when the spire was erected on the Rheatown United Methodist Church, from proceeds earned by selling the book, **Rheatown**.

RHEATOWN

1771 - 1977

Research, organization, securing material and information, and setting it up in proper order was no small task; and errors may occur. Much care has been taken to reduce them to a minimum. We ask your indulgence if any such error should affect you.

Sponsored by RHEATOWN UNITED METHODIST WOMEN

To Sue Piper Thomas, who spent time in researching and writing articles for this book. Now in her eighties and a newspaper woman for sixty-three years, she has deep roots in Rheatown where she lived, married, and where a part of her heart has always remained. For her kindness, patience and knowledge we feel a deep sense of indebtedness and are indeed grateful.

To Helen Thomas McCurry, who has given so unselfishly of her time for the past three years, researching to obtain material for the writing of this book. Helen is a four-generation member of the Rheatown United Methodist Church. Her love for this Church has been instilled in her through her grandfather, James R. White; her mother, Lulu White Thomas; her aunts, Minnie White Keebler and Franke White Denny. She has attended this Church all her life; and since uniting with the Church in 1940, she has held almost every office in the church. Helen is an excellent teacher of Methodism and the Bible. Presently she is teacher of the Junior Class, Church Pianist, Chairman of Worship, and Treasurer of United Methodist Women.

With the printing of this book, Helen is seeing a dream come true. Hopefully with the selling of the book, her second dream of a new spire for the Rheatown United Church will become a reality.

The Rheatown United Methodist Women are indeed grateful to this Christian lady.

(Appreciation and acknowledgement page from original printing in 1977)

CONTENTS

FOREWORD

This is the story of Rheatown, Tennessee, located in the upper east end of Greene County. It is written for the descendants of the early settlers and for those before the turn of the century, as well as for those born much later to let them know what it was like to have lived in the early years.

The original Rheatown came to an end shortly after the turn of the nineteenth century. You will never know what it was like firsthand, and you will never know the country from which your forebears came and founded the early settlement. You might recognize from hearsay and legend a very few houses, or a hill or stream that still exists; but one thing you will never find is the atmosphere that pervaded the area as it was many years ago. The rest has vanished. Only a few descendants reside in the area. Many live in various parts of the United States, having migrated to greener fields. One thing that still exists is the main street on the old stage coach road leading from Washington, D.C., to Nashville, Tennessee, which time and modernization have altered.

Rheatown is the story of a way of living which has largely gone out of fashion. We admonish you to cherish this story. It has been condensed in order to give you some of the high points of the past. The early settlers had two fundamentals which once were and still remain to be intensely American characteristics — integrity and idealism.

This story is sponsored by the United Methodist Women of Rheatown United Methodist Church. Read it and picture yourself as living in those early days.

(Foreword from original printing in 1977)

THE STORY OF RHEATOWN

Residents of Rheatown, Tennessee, observed two special historic events in 1976 — the 200th birthday anniversary of the United States of America as an independent nation and the 205th anniversary of the beginning of the settlement of Rheatown. The first settler arrived in the area between 1771 and 1772. Others followed closely thereafter.

Projects of the Rheatown United Methodist Women for the double celebration include the restoration of the belfry and steeple of the Rheatown United Methodist Church and publicizing the history of the settlement from its early beginning to the present time.

The story — a fascinating one — offers residents and descendants of the early pioneers living here and elsewhere the opportunity to review its glorious past and its contribution to the nation's heritage. Its history reflects the fact that from thirteen weak and independent colonies was formed one of the strongest nations in the world.

Rheatown, situated in the upper east end of Greene County on the old stage coach road leading from Washington, D.C., to Nashville, Tennessee, was not only the oldest and largest settlement in Greene County at the time, but is referred to by many historians as the second oldest in the East Tennessee area — Jonesborough being the oldest.

Rheatown was doomed in later years when the East Tennessee and Virginia Railroad was built, bypassing it by about a mile. It is now known as the Southern Railway. In 1865, the first train was operated from Bristol to Knoxville. Because it was built on land owned by James Fullens, the station was known as Fullens for a number of years. The name was changed to Chucky, later spelled Chuckey — a name believed to have originated from the Indian vernacular.

On the day the first run was made, many settlers for miles around gathered at the various stations along the route to view the sight. A great aunt of mine, the late Mrs. W.T. Mitchell (nee Ann Piper), rode the train from Knoxville to this area. She was born in Rheatown, the daughter of Albert M. and Martha Piper. Her parents moved to Knoxville when she was ten years of age. Her father was mayor of Knoxville at one time. Her parents are buried in the Rheatown cemetery.

In 1855, the celebrated American historian, George Bancroft, who had been a member of President Polk's cabinet, visited this area, coming by horseback through southwest Virginia. He was on his way to deliver the historical address at King's Mountain at the celebration of the battle fought there October 7, 1780. He was charmed by the town and predicted great things for it.

Early settlers were of the Anglo-Saxon race, English, Scotch and Scotch Irish. The Scotch Irish came largely from four counties of Northern Ireland, having descended from the English and Scotch planted there by King James I.

They were God-fearing. They would not intermarry with inferior peoples; they believed in separation of church and state; if abused they would fight; if their liberties were infringed upon and threatened, they would rebel; if forced they would strike and even murder, but murder was never in their hearts. They liked good food — especially meat — and they wanted their bread hot.

When the early settlers arrived in this area, they found to their surprise plenty of wildlife. The soil was rich and there were seven large springs, as well as a creek running through the settlement.

Among the early settlers were James Allen, a merchant who was succeeded by Joseph and Nicholas Earnest; Joseph Whinery, a hatter; William Aiken, a tanner; Thomas and William Handley, tailors; John A. Mathes, a cabinetmaker; and John Wright, a grist- and sawmill operator. Others who arrived about the same time were the Bandys, Likens, John Rankin, Ezra Pierce, Jeremiah Jack and John Rhea.

John Rhea was one of the foremost leaders among the pioneers. He came to the settlement in 1783, entering the area through the second gap of McCarty Mountains, later known as Quaker Knobs. He stopped at the big spring and built his cabin in the center of town. Born in Ireland in 1753, he was the eldest son of Rev. and Mrs. John Rhea. He was graduated from Princeton University in 1789. He and his father were noted Greek scholars, and while in General Washington's army they corresponded in Latin.

As a student of law, Rhea assisted in the organization of the State of Tennessee and the writing of the state's constitution. By this time he had moved to Sullivan County and was chosen the first representative from that county to the state legislature.

When Tennessee was divided into congressional districts, he was elected to Congress from the First District, where he served with distinction. He was in the confidence of three Presidents. When Governor Blount took office September 20, 1790, his name was among the lists of early appointments made by Blount.

During the Revolutionary war, he was a staff officer. In 1771 he was selected clerk of North Carolina General Assembly. At that time, this entire area was known as Washington District, the first section to be named for the first president of the United States. While a clerk in the Carolina Assembly, he had a new act enacted, carving Sullivan County out of a portion of Washington County. Two years later he was returned to Congress. He retired at the end of the term. He was a Jeffersonian Democrat and a special friend of Andrew Jackson. He was never married; and when he died in 1839, he left a large estate in land, most of which was grants for special services rendered.

It was during his last term in Congress that he obtained a post office for this area. That was in 1823, and because he had done so much for the village, the post office and town was named Rheatown.

The post office was operated until the rural delivery service was inaugurated. Just who the first postmaster was is not known. After the post office was eliminated, a sub-station was operated for the convenience of the residents for a number of years. Only stamps and money orders were sold. Part of the time they were obtained in J.D. Keebler's store, and at one time William F. Piper sold them from his giant print shop located in a small room attached to the log house formerly owned by a Clawson family. The William F. Piper family lived in this house until a new one was built next to it.

Among the early mail carriers from the Chuckey Post Office were James Peters, who resided between Rheatown and Chuckey. Thomas McAdams of Rheatown served as his assistant. Later carriers included Robert Ackard, William G. Slagle, Earl White, and Walter Balding. For many years Lawrence Bradley and Willie Armstrong were carriers on the Star Route from Chuckey Post Office to Jearoldstown. The present carriers through Rheatown are Wade Collette on route two with Argel Ripley substitute. Jack Grubbs is on route one with Rev. Jimmy Bowers serving as his substitute.

Although Rheatown was a thriving town, it was not until the first session of the Thirty-first General Assembly of Tennessee in 1856 that an act was passed to incorporate it. Section 15, Chapter 267 set forth that the governing body should consist of a mayor and alderman. Section 16 of the same chapter designated the town's limits, with section 18 citing that the chapter of the incorporation was the same as that adopted for Greeneville in 1846. It also provided for selection of officers. The identities of these first officers are unknown.

The first mayor of whom the residents have any knowledge was Joe D. Keebler, who was not elected until sometime later after the close of the Civil War.

In 1905 Monroe J. Reams, retired engineer from Knoxville, married the widow of Reese Thomas, Martha Baxter Thomas, and moved to Rheatown. In 1906 Mr. Reams was elected mayor.

For sometime before the turn of the century and shortly thereafter, the town was active with a lot of work accomplished. Mr. Reams was in charge of having

Monroe J. Reams, who was elected Mayor of Rheatown in 1906. He was married to Martha Baxter and is buried in Old Gray Cemetery, Knoxville, Tennessee.

MAIN STREET OF RHEATOWN *This picture was taken just east of the creek near the Shoun or J. Newt Range house in 1890. In the foreground is the Tannery, run by Jim Russell. The second building on the left is J.J. Marshall's Drug Store. Beyond and out of view is Keebler's Store and the Odd Fellows Lodge Hall. On the right foreground is Wilson's and Fisher's Blacksmith Shops, Finkle's Store, Thomas' Hardware & General Store, Cox's Boarding House, Cox's Inn, and the Bob McAdams House. Barely in view are the Post Office and Print Shop. The Rheatown creek can be seen crossing the street from right to left. This portion of Rheatown was a scene of great activity at the turn of the century.*

—4—

street lights installed and appointing a lamp lighter. Lude Laughlin, a black man, was responsible for lighting the lamps at sun down and extinguishing them in the morning. He also kept them cleaned and filled with kerosene, using a step ladder to reach them.

Alex Moody and Will (Billy) Babb served as policemen when Mr. Reams was mayor. They wore uniforms just like the city policemen of that period.

William F. Piper served as alderman at one time. The date he was elected is unknown.

Rheatown was never planned for a town, but some of the early pioneers must have envisioned it as a good place to settle, and for a time it boomed. The homes and cabins lined both sides of the old stage coach line, with streets opening up toward Chuckey and the Quaker Knobs. Like most early villages, the houses were set near the long wide streets. The business houses were also on the main thoroughfare. Unlike a lot of new settlements, residents were unwilling to make out with mud when it rained, and dust when it was dry. They banded together and paved the main street with large flat limestone rocks leading from the old Bright store to the Presbyterian Church at the top of the hill going east. A rock sidewalk was laid from the Robert McAdams house to the Presbyterian Church. A board sidewalk was built later on the opposite side of the street. A board walk was also built on the left side leading to Chuckey. It started at the Squibb house opposite the present United Methodist Church and ended near the Rheatown Academy.

The old stage road, which was the major thoroughfare connecting the eastern cities with the South and Southwest, ran through Rheatown. After leaving Jonesborough, the road continued through Leesburg and Rheatown and Greeneville.

Rates of Fare
From Jonesborough to Rheatown $1.00
From Rheatown to Greeneville   .75
(**Knoxville Gazette**, October 6, 1792)

Rheatown was a major stopping point for the stage coaches. The late Mrs. Clara Winslow Range's great grandfather kept supplies for repair of the coaches. His shop, located to the east of a farm near the U.M. Bradley farm, was the stopping place for repair work. Because of the rough roads, repair work was nearly always necessary. A stable for exchanging the tired coach horses for fresh ones was located just one mile east on what was known as the Berry Miller farm, later known as the Fletcher Dotson farm. The stage coach made two trips weekly from Washington to Nashville. One of the drivers was William (Billy) Bolinger who lived in Rheatown. He was the father of Henry Bolinger and grandfather of J. Allen Bolinger of Kingsport and the late Willie Bolinger of Rheatown. He has many descendants living in and near Rheatown.

For weary travelers Rheatown afforded a well-kept hotel. The hostelry was operated by a Mr. McKay at one time. Later it was known as Cox's Inn. It was operated by Dr. Cox and his son Dick. His widow, with the assistance of her daughter, Fanny, managed it in later years. The building was a large two story frame structure.

Throughout the earliest years of the village, many celebrities were entertained here, many of them during the stage coach era and others much later. Bancroft, the great historian, stopped in the village. In passing through town, the noted Jesse James stopped for the night.

On one occasion James K. Polk, who later became President of the United States, spoke in the village. Andrew Jackson once stopped here enroute to his home in Nashville. The late and beloved Alfred Taylor of Happy Valley in Carter County visited this area on several occasions when he was electioneering for a seat in the Tennessee House of Representatives, and again when he was elected to Congress, a post he held for three terms. He also stopped here when he was elected Governor of Tennessee.

For many years, the story was told about the day Andrew Johnson spoke in Rheatown. A short time before he was to address a large crowd, he stopped at the home of a friend and said, "I heard you have in your house a keg of good French brandy. I have come to see if I could get a big snort to warm me up to make my speech." The brandy was forthcoming and the Great Commoner was "het" up for the occasion.

The Cox Inn had ceased operation long before the building was destroyed by fire in 1913, along with a dwelling house and the old brick store from which Major R.H.M. Donnelly sold goods for a long time.

The late Mr. and Mrs. J.D. Keebler operated a stopping point for the old-fashioned traveling salesmen, better known as "drummers". Mr. Keebler operated a general store across from his home. They were known as Uncle Joe and Aunt Sarah. The drummers would travel several miles just to spend the night and consume some of Aunt Sarah's good meals. In time, she learned to know which dishes to fix for each one, as well as when certain drummers would be arriving. For several years, Bob Cooper of Greeneville would arrive every Monday to spend the night. One salesman wanted blackberry pie for breakfast, and it was ready for him. As times and customs changed, many did not come as often, but there

McAdams House   Cox Inn

The Bob McAdams family owned and occupied this house for many years. Since the death of the McAdams family, several other families have lived there for short periods of time. In 1948-49 Rev. and Mrs. W.D. Tranbarger and family lived there. The house has since been demolished.

Joe Keebler House

were a few who never stopped coming. The day before Uncle Joe died in 1938, one came by and spent the night. He returned early the next afternoon to see if there was anything he could do to help the family.

If anyone needed a lawyer back in the earlier days one was available. He was A.N. Shoun. Shoun was born in Johnson County in 1851, the son of G.H. and Thesdosia Wilson Shoun. They moved to Rheatown when A.N. was thirteen years of age. In 1865, he attended Emory and Jefferson College in Knoxville; he had one year of schooling at Rheatown Academy, and completed school at Emory and Henry College in Virginia in 1873. That same year he was married to Kate Johnson, daughter of Thomas Johnson. They had four children. Later he moved to Greeneville where the law firm was known as Ingersoll and Shoun. Several persons in this area read law under him.

Many descendants of the early settlers moved to other areas, where they held responsible positions. Their children and grandchildren are to be found in every state of the union.

John Hixon, son of the Methodist minister, Rev. J.D. Hixon, went to Oklahoma where he held a responsible position until he retired. The family resided in the Methodist parsonage for many years while Rev. Hixon pastored the Rheatown Church. John was well liked in the community. He came back for vacations for many years and was always made welcome by his many old friends.

Will Bennett was another hometown boy who made good in the big city. He was married to Mattie White, daughter of Isaac and Elizabeth Morley White. They moved to Washington, D.C., where he opened an insurance office. His business was a success. He raised his family there and continued in the insurance business as long as his health permitted. One daughter, Mrs. Walter Manner (Ina), now resides in Chevy Chase, Maryland.

In 1869 Mr. and Mrs. W.C. Snapp moved to Rheatown and bought a farm. Their son, R.J. Snapp, managed the farm from 1872 to 1876. He then went to Greeneville and built Snapp's Opera House. It was considered to be the most glamorous of any in that town for years. The auditorium was on the second floor. The first floor was used for stores and shops.

The sterling qualities of the pioneers of Rheatown constitute an historical fact in which the later inhabitants of this area in all time to come may take pride. Some of them have always done the one great thing in every crisis. They followed through on the tradition as the Volunteer State. They have battled in all the wars and they have been just as quick to fight for peace.

When the call came for volunteers in the Spanish-American War, several applied for enlistment but were rejected. Those that went to battle were Ruble Bailes, Alex Moody, Joe Shields and Randolph Scott. They all returned home.

In World War I, one of our beloved boys, Henry White, son of James R. and Mary Good White, failed to return. He was killed in France. His body now lies on home soil in Rheatown Cemetery. The story of the Civil War is contained in another chapter of this history.

Modern improvements were slow in reaching the little village. For many years, there was only one telephone in town — that was in the J.D. Keebler store. Later Monroe J. Reams had one installed in his home. Later Will and Frank Fisher had one installed in their store.

The first general improvement made in the town was the paving of the roads. That was several years ago. When the paving was done, bridges were built over

John Rowe's Jitney

Rheatown Food Market

Country Convenience Store

the creek. The old scales on which cattle and other farm products were weighed was removed.

In the early 1920's Rheatown had bus service when Big John Rowe made two round trips daily between Chuckey and Greeneville in his Jitney Bus. The fare was fifty cents a round trip. Big John had a flourishing business. The bus was usually filled to capacity.

Rheatown today is a growing residential area with a population of one hundred fifty-three, within the city limits. Many retired citizens, including a number of school teachers, reside in this quiet, peaceful settlement and surrounding area. The retired teachers include: Fleta Jeffers Kenney, Mildred Bowman Jeffers, Ollie Rosnick Ball, Selma Hankal Ricker, Ruth Grant Duncan, Mildred McLain, and Helen Thomas McCurry. Many changes have been made in the village in recent years. Numerous modern homes have been built and many of the old ones restored and modernized.

Rheatown boasts two lovely United Methodist Churches which share the same pastor, Rev. Harry Thomas. The parsonage is located next door to the Albright Methodist Church.

The residents have the convenience of two food markets. Craig McCurry and James Treadway operate the Rheatown Food Market and modern laundromat in their establishment. Recently Mr. and Mrs. Bill Runyan finished construction of a modern market, ''Country Convenience Store''. This market stands on the site of the old Oscar Wolfe store. Mr. Wolfe's store burned in 1974. At the time it burned it was operated by his brother, Ralph Wolfe.

Other businesses include an engine repair shop and a piano shop. Bo Cooley and Charles Scott operate a small engine repair shop in the little brick house that was once used as a hat shop. The piano shop is owned by Carroll Fletcher. Mr. Fletcher is the only qualified technician in the area and is kept very busy as a result. He also rebuilds organs and pianos and is technician for Roy Acuff of The Grand Old Opry.

Fletcher Piano Service

A portion of the 11-E highway will pass through the community, giving residents quick and easy access to Greeneville and Johnson City.

Rheatown is a charming town any season of the year, but it is especially beautiful in the fall when the trees in the village and the surrounding knobs are dressed in their brilliant colors of every hue. Many people drive through the village and the gap of the Quaker Knobs just to view this spectacular sight.

THE KEEBLER HOUSE *This house was built by a Mr. Squibb. It was later occupied by the Joseph Barnes family. The next owner was Henry Bolinger; his son J. Allen was born there, March 10, 1909. James (Jim) Keebler was the next owner. The house is located directly in front of the Rheatown United Methodist Church. It has a gabled roof with vertical board exterior. It has a stone foundation and a nice cellar with a dirt floor. It is one of the few houses in Rheatown that has a bay window. This house is in excellent state of repair and is owned and occupied by Viola and John Adams.*

THE SAMPSON HOUSE *Melissa Sampson's house was a three story gabled house that had a lot of gingerbread trimming on it in its younger days. Some people in Rheatown thought this house was haunted. Mrs. Sampson, the widow of Civil War veteran Ward Sampson, raised her family here. Raleigh Ricker and his wife, Selma, now live in a neat bungalow on this site.*

THE MONK HOUSE *This house which still stands on the road between the gap of the Quaker Knob and the Quaker Knob Church has been remodeled into a modern house, but it still carries the basic lines of its first construction. The Charles Monk family own and occupy this house at the present time.*

THE WILSON HOUSE *This is a small two story house with windowed gables that make it a very pretty structure. Since Mr. Wilson's death this house has been occupied by the families of Clyde Waddell, Will Fisher, Clyde Fisher, Tom Hudson and the late Mrs. Rosetta Dickson and perhaps other families. This house is in good condition and is owned by Joyce Click Smith.*

THE EARNEST HOUSE *This house was built before the Civil War. It is built of handmade bricks and is a very fine and sturdy structure. The mortar used to lay the brick was made of sand and home-burnt lime. This house originally had slave quarters built on the back. It was later known as the Jack White House. The present owner is Edward Lamons.*

MANUFACTURING
by
Sue Piper Thomas

It was not long after the Rheatown settlement was started until other people began obtaining land throughout the area for farms. By that time, the town had become almost indispensable to most sections of Greene and Washington counties.

The period following the destruction and disturbance of the Civil War was one of industrial progress throughout the country. The trend was reflected in Rheatown by the establishment of many small scale manufacturing plants.

Goodspeed, the noted historian, wrote in 1887 that William Aiken, one of the earliest settlers, built a tanyard near the creek. Either before or soon after, C.G. Rankin built a tanyard nearby. He tanned beef hides and deer skins — one half for the other. It is said that this tanyard was operated for over a hundred years by a Mr. Chandler, Ham Shoun and Jim Russell — the latter a well-to-do black man. It was located on the right hand side of the street going east. Russell was tanning hides there during World War I. Portions of the old vats can still be seen. (See picture, page 4.)

At one time, Mel Squibb owned a tanyard below the one that Russell operated. Squibb had a shoe shop where he converted the leather into shoes. He employed several people. Among them were Marion Testament, Whit Morrison and Pegleg Collins. John Grey was a shoemaker and lived in Rheatown. Where his shop was located is not known.

Jim and Bob Conn had a shoe shop directly across the street from Squibb. They had a tanyard in Walkertown and worked their leather into shoes and boots. A father would measure the feet of his children and take the measurements to them. The shoes were all black, hard and stiff.

They were put together with little wooden pegs. Every child that wore them really hated them. The late J.J. Marshall said he wore a pair of their shoes when he was graduated from Tusculum College in 1888. These shoes were made by Bill Rupe. Bud Leibs and Bill Rupe worked for the Conns for years. Joe Bales was another cobbler in Rheatown. Later he moved to Jonesborough where he plied his trade to a ripe old age. It was said at the age of eighty-nine he was still going strong.

Soon after the Civil War a Mr. Pierce established a carriage shop. This art represents a much higher degree of craftsmanship than making wagons. He is reported to have made the best buggies, hacks, and carriages in the East Tennessee area.

William McKeehan manufactured a chaffpiler threshing machine. It was the pioneer of the modern machine. The chaff, wheat, and straw all came out together. The power was furnished by horse power and transferred to the thresher by means of a tumbling shaft with knuckle coupling. The shafts were in three sections — two of iron and one of wood. The machine was hauled from farm to farm in a wagon.

Along with the threshing machine went the windmill or fan made by Tom Doyle.

The fan was almost identical with the cleaning apparatus used in the modern machine today, except it was worked by a crank. The Doyle farm was at the foot of McCarty Mountain. The farm is now owned by the Denver Bowers family.

Furniture and coffins were two other industries. Joe Collins and Joel DeBusk were the first cabinet makers. They made all kinds of furniture for the home. Some of the furniture is still being used in homes around Rheatown.

The late Tom Collette once owned a pair of bedsteads made by DeBusk. They also made coffins out of the finest walnut lumber. Mr. Collins moved to Kansas and Mr. DeBusk died in Rheatown.

Major R.H.M. Donnelly and Gideon Burkhart were the owners of a fruit and berry evaporator. They would buy the products outright or dry them on the shares. The late Mrs. J. Newt Range said she picked many gallons of blackberries and sold them for five cents per gallon and thought she was making money. The dryer which was heated by a woodburing furnace was located near the home of the late Mrs. Earle (Lulu) Thomas. Shortly after the Civil War, a young Federal soldier by the name of Joseph B. Wilson came to Rheatown from Johnson County and began making the famous Wilson wagons. He also made caskets. He followed his trade as long as his health would permit. Mr. Wilson had his iron work done by blacksmiths, Major Scott, Bill Scott, and Bob Dukes. The blacksmith shop was located near the drive to the Reece Thomas home.

Several years later the lots were purchased by the late Earle Thomas and are now a part of the Thomas farm, now owned by Mrs. Guy Thomas.

About 1875 Patty Farris migrated here from Virginia and opened a tin shop. He made candle sticks, candle moulds, coffee pots, water buckets, and bread and cake pans. In fact he could make almost anything needed in tin. He would make up a lot of his wares, load them in a hack, and peddle them from door to door all over the countryside. He brought Oscar Lee with him as a helper. The late Vess Rhea was an apprentice in his shop. Rhea became an expert in tin craft. He later moved to Greeneville and established the Vess Rhea Tin Shop in which he worked until his death. The Rhea Tin Shop is still in operation.

There have been several blacksmith shops in Rheatown. Already mentioned above were the Scott men and Bob Dukes. Henry Fisher was another blacksmith. They were always busy men, making farming implements, shoeing horses, and repairing machinery and tools. The early ones also made many iron cooking utensils, such as spiders, skillets, pots, irons, etc. Many of these utensils are still used in the old homes in Rheatown.

Ed Dukes and a brother made wagons. Billy Dukes had a harness and saddle factory sometime during the 1870's and 1880's.

D.R. (David Reese) Thomas (grandfather of Helen T. McCurry), came to Rheatown from Jonesborough. He manufactured wooden one-horse rakes. This rake was all wood except the teeth, the seat, and the rims on the wheels. It is reported that one of these rakes is still being used by the Rader family of Dulaney, who also owns one of the Rev. James Fisher corn shredders.

James G. Fisher, a minister, invented and manufactured the hand-operated shredders. They were quite efficient, and many of them are still being used in

Greene County. Mr. Fisher's wife, Elizabeth, was also a kind of manufacturer. She had a large loom on which she wove carpeting. Families would prepare their own material, cutting worn material and other material into inch-wide strips and sewing them together. She wove them in yard widths and any length that was desired. Nearly everyone in Rheatown had one or more rooms covered with carpet woven by her.

One very popular item manufactured in the town was wool hats. Ezra Pierce, one of the early settlers, built a house astride the upper part of the creek, where he not only made the hats, but carded the wool to make them.

The wool was carded into folds some two feet long. Mrs. Pierce spun the wool into yarn, dyed it, and wove it into cloth. The hats were said to be far better than those made by John B. Stetson. The Stetson hats were said to wear out while those that Pierce made just went to seed. When they got to this point they were used as inner soles in shoes. The late J.J. Marshall said he and Charlie Argenbright wore one between them for years. Ladies' hats were woven of checked or striped linen — the linen being woven from flax. B.F. Whinnery worked in the hatter's shop for years. It is said that the Whinnery family had a hatter's goose which their grandfather brought from Ireland. Some old timers say that the "Little Brick" now owned by Bo Cooley was once a hatter's shop. Many families have made their home there since it was used to manufacture hats.

For several years Joe D. Keebler and son, James, operated a cannery in Rheatown. Beans and tomatoes were the principal crops canned. However, they did can some corn, sweet potatoes, and fruits. The cannery furnished employment for many people. The name *Keebler's Choice* was used for the tomatoes. During World War I, a young man went into an eating establishment in France. He looked up

The Cannery

and saw a can of *Keebler's Choice* on the shelf. He said to the waiter, "Let me have a can of those tomatoes. It's almost the same as being at home." He wrote Mr. Keebler a letter telling him of his find and enjoyment of the tomatoes. That was a few years after Mr. Keebler had closed the cannery. He also ran a grist mill — grinding meal and feed for cattle.

John Burnsides, a black man, had a broom factory. He could make any type of broom that people requested. They were considered the best brooms in the country. Nearly everyone raised some broom corn in their gardens to be used in their brooms. Often there was a surplus of the plant, which he would make into brooms and sell to outsiders. He was known to have shipped them out of the state, and lots of stores in Greene and Washington counties carried his brooms in their stock.

BURNSIDE HOUSE *This house stood where the main street of Rheatown turned south onto the Chuckey road. It was a dwelling home until around 1915 when a Negro by the name of John Burnside converted it into a broom factory and general repair shop. The locust tree beside the house was over one hundred years old. It was trimmed repeatedly but still it refused to die. Modern road-building finally took not only the tree but also the house.*

THE HENRY FISHER HOUSE *This is one of the many "L" shaped houses in Rheatown. Like most of them, it had what was known as gingerbread work on its trim, especially around the porch. This house is in good condition and is now owned by Frank Jeffers.*

THE CLYDE FISHER HOUSE *This house located on the Old 11-E Highway near Oakdale was first occupied by Mariam Brown, who was called the "Cat Woman" because she had so many cats. The Clyde Fisher family lived here for many years. It was later owned by Walter and Sue Blankenship. It has been remodeled and is now owned and occupied by Mr. and Mrs. Pollard Hice (Willie Blankenship).*

THE HIRAM FRAKER HOUSE *This house standing in the lower part of Rheatown was built by Mr. Fraker. Other families who occupied this house were Russells, Greenways, Neas, and Weems. Charlie Hayes purchsed this property in 1945. His daughter, Eula, and her husband, Daryl Collette, now own this property; and the house is in excellent condition.*

THE DAVE GRANT HOUSE *Located between Rheatown and Chuckey, this house has been vacant for several years. It has simple but beautiful lines of architecture.*

MERCHANTS

Rheatown has had a number of good mercantile establishments. The early stores carried most items that were available in those days. The shelves were stocked with items that were most needed and wanted. Farm people from far and near would load their wagons and hacks with farm products, drive to town and exchange them for merchandise.

Jim Duncan founded a store in the early history of the town. James Allen was another pioneer merchant. He was succeeded by Joseph and Nicholas Earnest. The latter Earnest sold his part to Joseph and became a farmer. Madison G'Fellers sold goods in the town. He had a thriving business in the years 1837 and 1838. John Campbell also sold goods here at one time.

C.G. Rankin was born March 5, 1837, in Rheatown. He was the son of John and Louisa Gray Rankin. He became a merchant and also operated a tannery.

In 1866, Henry G. Marsh opened a mercantile establishment, and after a period of time moved to another town where he continued his career as a merchant.

After the Civil War, Gideon Burkhart, father of Prof. Henry Burkhart, came to Rheatown from Washington, D.C., where he had been stationed in the Quartermaster Department of the Army. He formed a partnership with Hiram Fraker. A short time later, Major R.H.M. Donnelly purchased Mr. Fraker's interest. This firm did business for about 30 years. They bought just about everything anyone had to sell. This included live partridges, ginsing, feathers, dried apples and peaches, eggs, chickens, etc. Later, an evaporator was built to bleach the fruit and berries.

Major Donnelly was very popular and a great leader in his day. He was married to Eliza Allen of Greeneville. He not only had the largest store, but the largest family — 17 children in all. When Burkhart retired from the firm, Will Earnest, who married a granddaughter of his, became his partner.

Mr. Donnelly was first a lieutenant in the Federal Army then promoted to the captain. He was retired with the rank of major. He is said to have had a beautiful home, living where Alta Davis now resides. He owned a large fish pond which was stocked with carp by the late Major A.H. Pettibone, a big political figure at one time. When he retired from the mercantile business, he returned to farming in 1886, later moving to Chuckey, then known as Fullen's, where he operated the Donnelly Hotel. When it was destroyed by fire, he retired again, returning to Rheatown. He first resided on the Lewis property across from the cemetery. After the death of both Dr. and Mrs. J.R. Morley, he purchased their home and lived there until his death in 1927. He was nearly 93 years of age.

A second notable store was that of James H. Bright, later known as the J.D. Keebler Store. Mr. Bright owned a large farm in the Liberty Hill section of the county, and he also was a cattle dealer. Before the railroad was built through Chuckey, he drove large herds of cattle to the eastern market.

After Mr. Keebler took over the operation of the store, he bought all kinds of farm products. The store included the main merchandise area with a lumber room attached to one side. Large bins were built in it to store wheat, corn, millet, rye, etc. Underneath the rear end, a room held the large number of chickens purchased, most of which were shipped to the eastern market along with numerous crates of eggs. A little office room was built on the front of the lumber room.

During the Thanksgiving and Christmas seasons numerous turkeys, geese, and ducks were also sold. Winters at that time were much colder than the present, and the fowl kept well. The poultry was usually dressed and hung in the large smoke house next to the store and shipped the next day. Hogs were also killed and dressed for shipment.

There was a time when large flocks of turkeys were driven through the town to Chuckey for shipment. Sheep were also driven in like manner.

Mr. Keebler kept a well-stocked line of medicines, of course mostly patent medicines. He kept a supply of castor oil, calomel, paregoric, liniments, salves, and remedies for the stomach and bowels. In fact, he kept almost everything that doctors used in that day and time. Another thing he had in his possession was various kinds of forceps for pulling teeth. He was routed out of bed many, many nights to pull a tooth or get some needed medicine for the ailing. He would get out his pocket knife, cut around the gums, and yank out the tooth. So far as is known, there were no bad aftereffects.

For a brief period before Mr. Keebler retired from the mercantile business, Jack White became a partner. He lived in the old Joseph Earnest property in the east end of town with his wife and four children, Karl, Alva, Eula, and Faye. Mr. White continued the store until he became ill. He died in 1907.

Rheatown merchant, William Earle Thomas (1884-1925)

There was a time the store was vacant. The independent Order of Odd Fellows moved out of the original site onto the second floor of the store building next to the McAdams home. The next store operators were Frank and Will Fisher. Then for a brief time in the 1930's, Roe D. Shoun operated a store.

In the years 1837 and 1838, Madison G'Fellers sold goods in the town. He was said to have had a thriving business.

Here are some prices taken from an old account book dated Rheatown, Tenn., Saturday, July 29, 1837.

Ira Harmon - trimming for coat - $1.75; Isaac Fox - 5 lbs. coffee - $1.00, 3 lbs. sugar, .50; James Fox - 6 lbs. sugar - $1.00; John S. Scott - 1 doz. eggs

The building that housed the Odd Fellows Hall stood adjacent to the Rheatown Creek and was used as a lodge hall until the 1920's, when Will Fisher bought the property after the lodge interest moved and death lowered its membership. He remodeled it into a general store that handles many commodities, including a line of drugs that were prescribed by the local doctor, William Bright. The store changed hands after Will Fisher moved to Johnson City, and then burned in the 1940's. A modern market now stands on this site. This store had the first gasoline pump in Rheatown. The rear of the stone basement was used in the early days for a Calaboose, hence barred door and the sketches in this book. Also note the "stile" or "uppen" block in front for mounting horses, also the hitching post.

The IOOF Lodge was established in Rheatown in 1888. Charter members were: Harry Bird, J.D. Keebler, H.K. White, J.R. White, Stanley Smythe, Clifford Smythe, Joe Rowles, Azeriah Evans, Bob McAdams, Tom McAdams, and Capt. J.J. Marshall who was the first candidate initiated after the lodge was organized.

- .07; James Dukes - 1 lb. coffee - .25; Jefferson G'Fellers - 10 yds. bed ticking - $2.50, 1 silk hdf. $1.25, 1 lb. tobacco, .25, 1 pair suspenders - .19; Burton Johnson, by cash, .50; W.M. Fraker, 1 blackberry box, .13.

Among customers that day were George Maltsburger, James Allen, Col. D.R. Johnson, David Tullock, William Brown, Joseph Johnson, William Glaze, John Britton, James Click, Andrew Waddell, Joseph Earnest, Russell Royston, and Samuel Waddle.

Other regular customers shopping in the village that day included John Reeser, James Chedster, several of the Collettes, the Bales family, Rimels, Thompsons, Cannon, Swatzell, Weldon Burton, Greene Hundel, Squibb, A. G'Fellers, James O. Earnest, Lawrence Glaze, Sammie Stonecypher, W.H. Naff, Wm. Jordon, C. Howell, John Stokes, George Jennings, Thomas Gilton, John Lloyd, Jacob Ellis, and James Dotson.

Prior to the takeover of the Bright store by Mr. Keebler, Henry Earnest was

THE REECE THOMAS HOUSE *This house was built for Dr. J.J. Howell in 1876. It is a spacious house with nine large rooms. It has exterior chimneys which provide fireplaces in four rooms. Three of these rooms have cabinet mantels. This house has been in the Thomas family since 1890, when it was purchsed by Reece Thomas and was later owned by his son, Earle. It is now owned and occupied by Mrs. Guy (Irene) Thomas.*

Billie Richardson Store

a popular merchant in that building.

About 1885, Billie Richardson opened a store. He obtained a contract to sell chickens, eggs, and butter to the Slocum Restaurant in Atlanta, Georgia. This was a good source of income for the ladies and made Mr. Richardson a very popular merchant.

Reece Thomas came to Rheatown from Jonesborough as a representative of the Buckeye Farm Machinery Company. He was married to Martha Baxter, daughter of Samuel Baxter of Cedar Lane. They went to housekeeping in Jonesborough, coming to Rheatown about 1890. They had two sons, Earle and Buford, who were born in Jonesborough. The machinery shop developed into a hardware store. Mr. Thomas died in 1897. The sons took over the operation of his business with the assistance of an uncle, J.B. Baxter. Later, they operated a general merchandise store on what was called the Thomas corner. The store was then known as Thomas and Keebler — James G. Keebler having joined the firm. Keebler was a member of the firm just a short time. M.J. Reams came to Rheatown and married Thomas' widow. He joined the firm and the store became Thomas and Reams.

Another important store was Good and Johnson. W.D. Good, a former county court clerk of Greene County, and his brother-in-law, Jim Johnson, opened a new store in 1880. E. Hartsell Good, brother of W.D., bought out the firm and had a thriving business for many years. The Good men were the brothers of Mary Good White. Her husband, J.R. White was once a partner.

Jacob Finkle, a native of Russia, emigrated to the United States. He was accompanied by two brothers, Max and Louis. When they arrived in New York, they were told to go to Tennessee where there was a rich field for merchants. Max and Louis stopped in Chuckey and opened a store. A few years later, Louis returned to New York and Max opened a store in Limestone.

Jacob became the first and only Jew to settle in Rheatown. He traveled all over the country, carrying a pack on his back for a time, selling his wares from door to door. Later, he traveled in a T-model Ford. Sam Guire was his driver. In his travels, he met and married Alice Linebaugh of Baileyton.

Mrs. Finkle designed and made women's hats. She also did some sewing. She and Mr. Finkle lived in a house next to the Jim Fisher home in the eastern part of town. They opened a shop on one of the corners of the road leading to the Quaker Knobs. Mr. Finkle kept his supply of merchandise in the shop, and Mrs. Finkle also sold a few items in connection with her hatmaking. When they decided to go their separate ways, Mrs. Finkle and her children settled in Maryville, Tennessee, where her children are now residing.

Later known merchants that have served this area were: Henry Bolinger; Newt Range; E.E. Ripley; Viola Good; Jack Thomas, who later went into partnership with James Massengill; Jerry Thomas of Virginia; George E. Ball and Oscar Wolfe.

GROCERIES AND DYE STUFFS

We confidently believe it to be to your interest to call and examine our Stock before purchasing elsewhere.

To insure good and permanent custom we shall sell at a very low per cenum for Cash or good trade in prompt payment and also, to solvent men at the same rate on time - if required - with the contract being understood in all cases, that henceforth all claims will be due at the expiration of, and accordingly will draw interest from that date.

And whilst we express our thankfulness for your past patronage, we sincerely trust to merit a continued bestowal of the same, hoping thus to protect your interest as well as ours.

REEVE & EARNEST

RHEATOWN, TENNESSEE, October, 1859

Mrs. Cecil Smith of Afton, Tennessee, has the original of this store ad. It was handed down from her great-grandfather, William Smith, to her father, John C. Smith. The family came to Rheatown to do most of their shopping.

CHARLES HANKAL HOUSE *This house was moved from the top of the hill down to the road. It is said to have been built by Dr. J.R. Morley. It was occupied by the Hankal family for many years, and later by the Velt Hilton family. It is now owned and occupied by the Brownlow McIntosh family.*

THE ROME DONNELLY HOUSE *This house was built for Rome Donnelly and his family by Henry V. Bolinger in 1917. The Donnellys lived here until they moved to Idaho in 1930. The house has since been occupied by Mr. and Mrs. B. Chase, Gene Dunham Lawing, Martin Chandler, and others. It is presently owned by George Wampler. A near duplicate of this house was built for Dr. Wm. Bright about the same time. It is located a few hundred feet west of this house on the opposite side of the road. It is now owned by Elza Estepp.*

THE FRAKER HOUSE *The Frakers lived in this sturdy farm house and farmed the large acreage. Since the passing of Mrs. Emma Fraker and her nephews, Tull and Roe Shoun, the farm has changed hands several times and the house is now unoccupied. A portion of the Quaker Knob can be seen in the background.*

THE FRAKER BARN *This is a large barn with several stalls. It has room to hold an acre or two of tobacco, a standard crop around Rheatown. Much of the exterior of this barn is horizontal weather-boarding. This barn is still in use today.*

CIVIL WAR

When the Civil War erupted, strife and hatred burned the foundation of brotherly love. In some instances it was brother against brother. East Tennessee was a strategic battleground. There was never a battle in Rheatown proper, but for some time the contending forces went back and forth through the town.

One severe skirmish was fought on the northeast side of the town on October 11, 1863. One side was flanked on what was known for a long time as the Bill Church hill, now known as the Bill McCurry farm; the other side was stationed near the old Stage Coach Line across from the Rheatown Cemetery. Many soldiers were killed and many wounded. Bodies of many of the dead now lie in unmarked graves along the front of the Rheatown Cemetery.

Dr. J.R. Morley of Rheatown, although a Confederate sympathizer, tended the wounds of both Rebels and Yankees. The old brick Presbyterian Church and the old Methodist church were used as hospitals. A new church now stands where the Presbyterian was built. The old Methodist Church is gone and only a few bricks of the foundation can be seen as a reminder of the power of the gospel as the healer of wounds of war and strife.

THE PRESBYTERIAN CHURCH *Built in 1856 by the Presbyterians, this substantial brick church served as a hospital during the Civil War. Dr. J.R. Morley, a Rebel doctor, administered services to both Yankee and Rebel soldiers in this building. It has stately plastered columns in front and was built of handmade brick. It was later purchased by the United Brethren Church.*

The late Mrs. J.N. (Clara Winslow) Range had two brothers killed in the skirmish. They were buried on what is known as Winslow Hill. Mrs. Range, who died in 1971, was a good historian of the area and often recalled the happenings of past events. She had in her possession a small cannonball about as large as a hen egg. Many smaller cannonballs have been found on the same land, now owned by Mrs. J. Brown.

On or about September 2, 1864, an estimated 4,000 soldiers camped around Rheatown. This was the detachment that took part in the battle of Greeneville on September 4th when General John Hunt Morgan was killed. General Morgan had moved his forces into Greeneville.

The skirmish that preceded the one at Rheatown took place October 10, 1863 at Blue Springs in the Mosheim area. It was slow in developing because the Union forces were allowing time for Colonel Foster to encircle the Confederate lines and reach a position near Rheatown.

The fighting was severe on both sides. That night the Confederates retreated to Greeneville where another skirmish occurred with the Confederates winning, but they fell back towards Jonesborough. Then followed the skirmish at Rheatown.

When nothing could be heard of the fate of General Morgan, Col. H.L. Giltner directed Capt. J.J. McAfee to take four men from the Fourth Kentucky Regiment, along with several others, to proceed to Greeneville and ascertain the fate of General Morgan. They halted in Rheatown and awaited the return of the flag of truce. At midnight a courier from Capt. McAfee announced that General Morgan had been killed and that the body had been taken to the home of a Mrs. Williams. He was shot near what was known later as The Fox Hospital.

A dispatch was sent to his widow in Abingdon, Virginia. The dispatch read:

HEADQUARTER'S BRIGADE NEAR RHEATOWN, TENNESSEE
Spetember 4, 1864

Mrs. General Morgan
Abingdon, Virginia

With deep sorrow I have to announce the sad intelligence of your husband's death. He fell by the hands of the enemy at Greeneville this morning. His remains are being brought away under flag of truce. We all mourn with you in this great affliction.

Most respectfully,
H.L. Giltner
Colonel Commanding Brigade

Being short of supplies, the soldiers on both sides requisitioned everything loose they could find.

Rheatown did her part in furnishing soldiers to both sides. Among those serving the Confederacy were Mell Naff, Nat Campbell, Jim Johnson, Jim Conn, and John Byerly. The latter was killed in battle.

A greater number of Rheatown residents united with the Federal Army. Among them were Billy Argenbright, James M. Bailes, J. Mell Squibb, Jacob P. Hubbard,

J.B. Wilson, Will Leib, Gideon Burkhart, John Baker, Elisha Baker, Jerri McCaleb, Joe Collins, Hartsell Good, J.D. Keebler, R.H.M. Donnelly and Charles Wesley Piper.

Mr. Hartsell Good, father of the late Mary Good White, was killed in action and buried in National Cemetery in Nashville, Tennessee. Mr. Keebler died in 1938 as the last surviving soldier in Tennessee. Charles Wesley Piper, whose parents were Mr. and Mrs. Albert M. Piper, was commissioned a First Lieutenant in the Fourth Tennessee Infantry.

Mr. Donnelly and Captain R.H. Luttrel raised a company which became Company D, 13th Cavalry. He became a First Lieutenant, then a Captain, and was mustered out as a Major.

Among the officers serving in the Union Army from Rheatown community from 1861 to 1865 were Levi Pickering, Captain Co. E, 4th Infantry and Gus H. Winslow, 2nd Lieutenant, Co. A, 4th Division.

There were a lot of Greene County men listed in 1st Cavalry, especially Co. H.; 4th Cavalry, Co. K; and 4th Tennessee Infantry. There is a record in the Greene County Registrar's office of former Union Soldiers who registered their discharges after the war.

When it was learned that enemy soldiers were in the area, Dr. Morley's family fled across a ridge and hid in a cave until it was safe to return home. One day

THE DR. J.R. MORLEY OR MAJOR R.H.M. DONNELLY HOUSE *This house was built before the Civil War. It was a long sprawling house with many doors and windows. The roof sagged more than the sketch shows. In the 1920's it was surrounded by beautiful maple trees that were a blaze of color in the fall. Other owners were Joe Daugherty and Dan Britton. Miss Amanda and her brother Alex Jordan also made their home there for several years. A few years ago the house burned, and a modern brick home has been built where the historical old house stood.*

when the doctor was at home, some Union soldiers looted his house. Among the valuables taken was his watch. As they rode up to the house, he went upstairs and got his pistol. As he appeared in the doorway, a soldier shot at him and the bullet struck the door frame above his head.

It was customary during the war to hire a substitute if a soldier had the money or was physically disabled. A Mr. Fraker had a lame arm and hired a substitute. After the war ended, a party of men met him at a store and gave him a good beating with a buggy whip. He knew the men, one of whom was a relative.

During the battle on the outskirts of town, the women and children took refuge on a nearby knob. From the knob they sent signals from a large tree atop the knob. A small mirror was used to send the messages to their men so they would know they were safe.

Robert H.M. Donnelly (1835-1927)

PHYSICIANS
By
Sue R. Thomas

Until 1936, Rheatown was fortunate in having several good physicians. However, information is scarce about the earliest ones. A Dr. William Ellis, who is buried in the Quaker Knob Cemetery, is believed to be the first in the area. Since so many Ellises were listed as being active in the Quaker Church, he was probably among the group migrating into the area.

Another doctor was a Mr. Reaves, who lived and practiced medicine in Rheatown long before the Civil War, his services having ended about 1840 or 1845.

Dr. Minton, who was an uncle to President Hoover, studied medicine under Dr. Ellis. He later moved to Portland, Oregon.

The late John Bales, an elder in the Quaker Knob Church had a son, Sam, who became a doctor. He practiced in Newport.

Probably one of the best known and loved in the earlier days was Dr. J.R. Morley. About 1850 he came to the town from Mountain City, which was then known as Taylorsville in Johnson County. He practiced for about a year and then returned to Mountain City and married Rachel Donnelly. On his return to the old J.D. Keebler home, or to be exact the old Shoun house (which was torn down many years ago), they set up housekeeping.

Dr. Morley traveled far and wide, day and night, leaving word at each stop where he would make his next call. He had two diplomas, one from the Baltimore School of Medicine and one from a school in Philadelphia, Pennsylvania. He

Emma (Morley) Fraker (1854-1939), wife of Dr. W.E. Fraker and daughter of Dr. J.R. Morley and Rachel R. Donnelly Morley.

THE LEWIS HOUSE *The Lewis house stands on the Old Stage Road near where you turn to go to the Rheatown Cemetery. After the Lewis family moved away, Dr. William Bright bought the farm and lived there until his death in the late 1920's. Soon after Dr. Brights's death, his sister, Phronia, and her husband, Dr. Edward Jeffers, moved here from Baileyton. Several families have lived here since the Jefferses moved. The house is now owned and occupied by the William Knight family.*

continued his practice for some 25 years after the Civil War before retiring. For some time after he retired, people would go to see him about some illness. Mothers especially would take their children to see him.

Dr. Morley had one daughter, Emma Morley, who married Dr. W.E. Fraker and resided a short distance from town. His practice did not last very long because of a very severe injury he received in a wreck on the Southern Railway between Knoxville and Chuckey.

Reading was a hobby of Dr. Morley's. His favorite book was the Bible, of which he was well versed, having read and studied it through many times.

Dr. Joe Doyle read medicine under Dr. Morley and then went on to graduate from Vanderbilt University. He had a successful career, later moving to Lincoln, Nebraska.

Dr. J.J. Howell was another successful physician of Rheatown. A native of North Carolina, he was educated in Greeneville and received a degree from Tusculum College and Vanderbilt University. Dr. Howell began the study of medicine in 1874, establishing a practice in Rheatown in 1876. In the same year he married Sarah R. Leming, daughter of John Leming. They resided in what was known later as the Reese Thomas home. Dr. and Mrs. Howell were the parents of five children. Dr. Howell was a self-made man. He was a very temperate man, being a member of the Methodist Episcopal Church South and a Master Mason. His service in Rheatown covered a period of about 10 years. Howell then relocated

Dr. J.R. Morley (1830-1907) and wife Rachel Donnelly (1832-1913) with grand-daughter, Eulalee Shoun

in Tusculum and was followed by a Dr. Tucker, who served the area for seven years.

Both Dr. J.F. Arnold and Dr. R.O. Huffaker, who spent most of his life in Chuckey, doctored in this area at one time.

Probably one of the youngest doctors practicing in the area was Dr. W.M. (Billie) Bright. He and his wife, Opal, were from Baileyton. Both were very active in the community. They lived for a while in the old Presbyterian manse, later moving into their new home now owned by Elza Estepp. Their last home was the old Lewis home across from the Rheatown Cemetery on the old Stage Coach Line.

When Dr. Bright died, his brother-in-law, Dr. Ed Jeffers, moved into his home and took over his practice. Dr. Jeffers moved his family to Rheatown from Baileyton, where his practice was a father-son combination. His father had always planned to follow farming and cattle trading, but the loss of his three year old daughter, who died of diphtheria, changed his mind. He went to Louisville, Kentucky, and studied medicine, returning to join his son, Ed. In 1908, they formed a practice that defied bad roads and little to no communication other than word of mouth, and combatted epidemics of diphtheria, typhoid, pneumonia, influenza and other known killers of the day. The influenza epidemic during 1917-1918 led to trying times. They had many humorous and sad experiences, especially when they performed duties of dentists on their rounds.

Dr. Jeffers and his wife, Phronia, had a fine family of nine children, all proving to be assets to the Rheatown community. Fleta, the eldest daughter, a retired teacher, resides with her husband, George Kenney, in the old Painter home, formerly owned by the late Henry Bolinger. Willard resides near the Albright United Methodist Church. Della lives in Morristown where she has held a responsible position for years. Rex, a successful mortician, and Frank, who is affiliated with Magnavox Co., live in Greeneville. E.B. lives in Virginia where he serves as a United Methodist Minister, Clarice lives in Kingsport and Doris is in Florida. Ralph, a son, was drowned several years ago.

Dr. Jeffers died in 1936, again leaving Rheatown without a doctor. There was a Dr. McIntosh and his wife, who came here to live for a while, residing in the Walter Lilly house. He did not practice here but was known on occasions to have made emergency calls. For years now, the nearest doctors have resided in Limestone and Greeneville, with no service available in the homes.

THE PAINTER HOUSE *This house is a tall two story house with a stairway going up that makes a right turn without a landing. It was owned by Henry Bolinger from 1915-1919. It was vacant from 1919 to 1922, when the Bolinger family moved back into it. Later Dr. Ed. Jeffers purchased it; and it is now owned by his daughter, Fleta, and her husband, George Kenney.*

THE COUNTRY HORSE DOCTORS
by
Peggy McCurry Balding

In 1928 Rheatown became the home of W.D. (Bill) McCurry when he, with his wife, Florence, and son, O.L. (Jack) McCurry, purchased the Will Church property and moved here from Pleasant Vale. The McCurrys had two daughters: Roxie, who died at age three and Ella, who was married to Paul Maupin before the family moved to Rheatown.

Daddy Bill was a livestock dealer and a horse doctor. He had almost no formal education. He was making his own way when he was nine years old. His parents both died when he was a toddler and he lived with his grandmother until her death. Then he started trading horses; I guess this is where the horse doctoring got its beginning, because he knew how to take a plug and make a real horse out of it.

He drove mules and horses both to North and South Carolina. He was always joined by Bill Britton, Buford Thomas (my great uncle), and Roy Hunt on these drives. They would camp out all the way over and back. Daddy Bill would often tell how Buford was sitting around the campfire darning his sock, when he stuck his finger and he said, "What is home without a mother."

Daddy Bill never owned an automobile. He would either ride his black stallion "Fandy", or people with sick cows and horses had to come and get him and bring him back home. He would leave early in the morning, often not returning until late at night. One farmer would take him to his farm and another would go pick him up. This would go on all day, and most of the time seven days a week. I guess animals are just like a lot of people; they don't know when Sunday comes.

A lot of farmers were busy all week and would just wait until Sunday morning to get their doctoring done. Therefore Daddy Bill never had much opportunity to go to church, but he would stop at Sunday School and call my Mother to come out and he would give her an offering to be put in the "card class". He would attend revivals, funerals, and always go to the Christmas programs, but when his hair turned white he said it was caused from sitting in damp churches listening to long-winded preachers.

Daddy Bill had a wealth of knowledge, not only about horses, but about many things. He could teach you things about everyday life that you could never learn in school. When I was a little girl he would say, "Cowpuncher," (his nickname for me) "a good true friend that will stand by you is worth so much more than money."

He helped many a wayward boy who had nowhere to turn. He would bring them in from the stockpen, and his home was their home until they could do better. He had a special love for children, and on Sunday afternoon we would gather at his barn and he would saddle everyone a horse and let us ride all afternoon.

He loved a good time and was a very witty person. He liked to dance. He would walk in a store and pat "Buffalo Gal" on his hands and start doing the shuffle. He would dance at school entertainments; and his neighbor, Dave Grant, would pick the banjo. That pair could bring down the house.

Will Church House
(The weeping willow tree was destroyed by storm in 1977.)

Daddy Bill had a nickname for everyone he met. As he would be riding along the road on old Fandy or in a car, he would holler at everyone he saw.

He also liked to hunt, but he always believed you should kill only the animals you needed for food. He thought everyone should know how to ride a horse and shoot a gun. He taught me how to do both at a very early age.

With his great love for people, he enjoyed company; and Ma Curry never knew if she would have one or twenty-one for a meal because he would always ask everyone who was there at meal time to eat.

Daddy Bill was an ardent Democrat and was chairman of the 15th district of Greene County as long as his health permitted.

When his death came in June, 1959, my world was shattered because, never knowing my Grandfather Thomas, I thought he was the greatest grandfather that ever lived.

My father, Jack, helped his dad doctor and farm; and in 1930 he married Helen Thomas, also of Rheatown. After their marriage he was employed at Veterans Hospital, Mountain Home, Tennessee, until 1947 when he returned to the country to join his father and become known as the ''Cow Doctor''. Daddy always had a way with cattle, and if he had a choice he would doctor the cows and leave the horses to Doctor Bill. Along with his ''doctoring'', he farmed and traded cattle.

Daddy always maintained an interest in the betterment of the community. In the late forties he was accepted in the Aracana Lodge #489 Free and Accepted Masons, which he served as worshipful master twice. He was a charter member of the Chuckey Ruritan Club, working with this group to get city water through the Chuckey Utility District. He servd as District Chairman of the United Fund for several years. He was also interested in getting an association formed for the Rheatown Cemetery. He was maintenance treasurer of this group. He was always active in the Rheatown United Methodist Church, although he did not become a member until December 15, 1963.

He served on the church official board in several capacities. Being a Democrat, he tried his hand at politics, running for Division Road Commissioner once. At that time he was the only Democrat that had ever carried all Republican 15th District of Greene County, although he was unsuccessful in the Division. After Daddy Bill's health became poor, Daddy was elected and served as Democrat Party Chairman for the 15th District.

Daddy had a magnetic personality and a great love for life. He enjoyed people and had friends far and wide. He, like his father, liked to dance; and he always took part in talent shows and school entertainments. Charles Earnest would play *St. Louis Blues*, and Daddy would tap dance. They would get encore after encore. Daddy sang tenor, and sometimes at church I can still almost hear him when the choir sings "I Shall Sing the Wondrous Story".

Daddy was a gentle man but a very strong disciplinarian. He never spanked me, but he never had to; he just had to clear his throat and I knew what to do or not to do.

Fourth from left, William (Bill) Dobson McCurry, others unidentified

He and mother always welcomed all my friends into their home when I was a teenager, whether it was for a party or just a girlfriend to spend the night. They always saw to it that we had a good time and plenty to eat.

In 1950, Daddy started selling hail insurance, establishing his own agency, O.L. McCURRY INSURANCE AGENCY, which he operated until his death, April 15, 1976.

He had a special love for his grandchildren, Jimmy and Amy. When Jimmy was little he took him on trips which Jimmy still remembers. He was confined to his room when Amy was born, but he always enjoyed her playing around his room.

Daddy's illness kept him confined to his home for five years, but he always welcomed his friends and was cheerful and kept a very positive attitude. He told me one day that if he could live long enough, something would be discovered that would help him; and through our good friend, Chauncy Depew, we learned of surgery he could have in Boston, Massachusetts. After several conversations with the doctor in Boston, my mother, my aunt Ella Maupin, and Daddy left Tri-Cities Airport in April, 1974, not knowing if Daddy would live to make the trip or if his heart would be strong enough for him to have the surgery once they got there. Everything worked out fine and he enjoyed two more years with his family.

When his death came, we tried to accept it as a blessing because we knew he was approaching the time that he no longer could enjoy the life he lived.

With Daddy's death this was the last generation to carry the McCurry name, as his only son, William Earl, died in infancy.

Mattie Florence (Smith) McCurry (1884-1964)

RHEATOWN ACADEMY
by
Sue R. Thomas

Although Rheatown was a great trading center almost from the time the earliest settlers began moving into the area, there was never a school in the town proper until 1875.

The citizens saw the need to build a school in the town following the Civil War, with the Nolichuckey Lodge, No. 323, Free and Accepted Masons taking the initiative. The school was known as Rheatown Academy, with some calling it the Masonic Academy.

The building was erected on a tract of land donated by Esquire Ham Shoun. The brick two-story structure was sixty feet long and thirty-six feet wide. It was built by the famous brick masons, H.H. Huffman and W.P. Thompson. (W.P. was the father of the late Samuel Thomspon, who headed a school in Chuckey at one time. He later had charge of Indian Affairs for the United States Government in Washington, D.C.) The top floor was used as a meeting place of the Masonic Order, the lower floor being used for school purposes. It included two rooms and a large stage. Folding doors separated the two rooms, and when opened it was converted into an auditorium.

Mr. Fletcher was the first headmaster, leaving the school at the end of the year. He was succeeded by Prof. Henry McClister. He was a strict disciplinarian, never fearing to use the rod.

Mr. McClister had an eye for beauty. Under his supervision, maple trees were planted all over the grounds in a systematic manner. They were magnificent in both the spring and fall. One of the greatest things he accomplished was to have a row of shacks built along one side of the campus so that students living too far away could room, cook their own meals, and attend school. Many of his students went on to other schools of higher learning and received their college degrees. Mr. McClister left the academy at the end of his third year for a better position. He was considered a good instructor.

Among those attending school under his administration were Nick, Rhea, and D.L. Earnest; J.J. Marshall; Clark Williamson; R.K. Boyd; Dave Nelson; Florence McCaleb; Thomas Boles; Frank and Mack Reeser; Joe and Tom Doyle; and Mary S. Keebler.

The board of trustees selected Prof. J.C. Wright to succeed Mr. McClister. He was just the opposite of his predecessor. His administration was considered to be the best in the county at that time. One of his accomplishments was to inaugurate commencement exercises. For the first Baccalaureate, the Rev. Nat G. Taylor, a Methodist minister of great distinction, delivered the sermon. He was a member of the famous Taylor clan in Happy Valley in Carter County. Major A.H. Pettibone, a noted political figure, delivered the commencement address.

Family names listed on the school roster for 1890 included Bailes, Baker, Campbell, Fisher, Grant, Jenkins, Keebler, McKeehan, Moody, Rowles, Rothrock, Scott, Sampson, Squibb, Shoun, Shields, Wilson, Yokley, Argenbright, Collette,

Rheatown Academy (1875-1915)

Cox, Doyle, Johnson, McCaleb, Rupe, Rankin, White, Whinnery, Hickson, Hyder, and Hubbard.

Prof. Wright left Rheatown to go to Chuckey to teach. His successor was A.M. Mettetal. Other teachers over the years included W.H. Armitage, J.R. Doty, John Carson, and W.F. Piper.

Mr. William F. Piper's teaching career covered a period of twenty to twenty-five years. Rheatown was among his first schools after graduating from Tusculum College in 1888 along with the late Capt. J.J. Marshall. He taught until entering his newspaper career in 1909. Other places he taught were Chuckey, Clear Springs, Liberty Hill, Newport, and a school in the mountains where they could not keep a teacher.

According to an old register, his students in Rheatown included Cleo Argenbright; Mabel Buck; Ella and Carrie Baskett; Willie and Lillie Bolinger; Gladys, John, and Hubert Baker; Willie Bales; Clayton Babb; James and Jodie Barnes; Lillie Maude and Lizzie Baxter; May and Frank Campbell; Homer Church; Edith and Willie Collette; Lee, Clifford, and Mauveline Dukes; Ollie and Frank Fisher; Campbell Fisher; Gladys Finkle; Willie, Clara, Annie, and Lillie Grant; Rosie King; Irene Keebler; Clara Keebler; Mary House; Alma, Clay, Justin, Hazel, and Pauline Myers; Carl McAmis; Randall Moody; Sue, Joe, and Rachel Piper; Tom and Ruth Rupe; Pearle, Frank, and Davie Smith; Buford Thomas; Alva, Faye, and Eula White; Franke, Henry, and Carl White; and Elsie Yokley. Eight of this group of Professor Piper's students became teachers. They were Clara Grant; Irene Keebler; Pauline, Hazel, Justin, and Alma Myers; and Faye and Eula White.

One school Mr. Piper taught in Rheatown was attended by a group from Pleasant Vale. Mrs. Mattie Loyd rented a house from J.D. Keebler in which were housed two of her daughters, a grandaughter, and a friend of her family, Myrtle Hunt.

Joseph H. Maupin, another efficient teacher of Rheatown Academy, was admired by his students. Later he ended his teaching career and was elected Greene County Court Clerk. He served in this office several years before he was elected Greene County Judge. After his retirement he lived on his farm in the Pleasant Vale community until his death.

Miss Caroline Donnelly, Hubert Kilday, and Mrs. Ben (Maude) Gregory were the last teachers. Mrs. Gregory was the teacher when the school building was destroyed by fire of unknown origin in 1915, thus ending the last school in the town. Mrs. Gregory finished out the school year teaching in her home. The county refused to build a school in Rheatown and the children were sent to Chuckey where they have been attending ever since.

D.D. Alexander made this comment about the Rheatown Academy in his last historical article which was published in the **Greeneville Sun.**

Rheatown Academy was at one time one of the best schools in the whole county. This school was taught in a large brick building which stood over the hill east of town. It was a large school and they advertised extensively in the old Greene County Fair catalog. They said you could obtain board in the very best of families at $1.50 per week. The building was finally destroyed by fire in 1915.

In its day it was one of the Professor Sam Thompson kind of schools. They used the old Blue Back Speller, and McGuffey's Reader and Davis Arithmetic. They also taught spelling and penmanship. In my opinion, two of the most essential things in any person's education.

I am sure Sam Thompson attended school in this old academy. In the schools of Greene County is where he learned we needed a better school system. When he completed his education he went to work to improve the school system. He stood for better school houses, a better system of study, better books, better teachers, and everything else that went for better schools.

Born three or four miles south of Rheatown, he was just a big hearted man. His work here will long be a matter of history.

Two years after the school house burned officers of the Masonic Lodge sold the school lot to Nathan Phillips for two-hundred dollars. The warrantee deed was made and notarized by James R. White, notary public, on May 25th, 1917. Henry and Georgia Ball purchased the land several years ago and built a modern home on the front of the lot. Several of the beautiful maples planted by Prof. McClister and his boys are still standing.

NOLI CHUCKEY MASONIC LODGE
Rheatown, Tennessee

Noli Chuckey
Greene County, East Tennessee
No. 323 A. F. M.
Slated meetings 1859

January 6	July 7
February 3	August 4
March 3	September 1
April 7	October 6
May 5	November 3
June 2	December 1
September 1	

September 1
Signed   William D. Good

This notice to the members of the lodge was found in Captain J.J. Marshall's scrapbook, written on a picture post card.

WILL BROWN'S SCHOOL WAGON *Few people around Rheatown remember the school wagon. Will Brown drove this enclosed hack, or surrey, from Clear Springs to Chuckey High School before there were modern school busses in Greene County. We pay tribute to this fine man, who was so faithful to an unglamorous job.*

RECREATION IN THE EARLY DAYS

Tusculum College commencement was always a big attraction. Those that did not intend to attend the event would rise early, do their work, and be ready to watch the buggies, carriages and hacks pass by. Lots of people took their lunches with them and spread it on the campus and there would be stands supplying various things to eat and drink. Those were big affairs in that time.

Shortly after the turn of the century, Rheatown had a ball team made up of young men from Rheatown and Chuckey. They belonged to one of the leagues at that time and traveled extensively. Buford Thomas was pitcher for the team. One time they made a trip to Spartanburg, South Carolina. Clarence ''Red'' Walker played with them. He at one time played ball with the Boston Red Sox.

Another big event attended by the local folks was the Sulphur Springs Camp Meeting. It was sponsored by the Methodists and attracted hundreds from all sections. For years it lasted for two weeks. Cabins were built for those who wanted to stay full time. Well-known ministers from various sections preached. It was organized in 1845 and is still going strong. It is now a three day meeting.

The young people for several years attended folk dances in the various homes. Candy pulling was great fun, especially in the fall when molasses boilings were held. The young people went often to the Major Scott's home to play croquet during the summer months. Another thing they liked to do was to congregate and go walking. Lots of times there was something doing at the Quaker Knobs. During those early years they thought nothing about walking several miles to a revival in the outlying sections. On a hot Sunday afternoon one could always find a crowd sitting around the big spring in the center of town. This spring was called the Shoun Spring.

In the earliest days of the settlement, there were apple butter stirrings, quilting bees, corn huskings, and benefit ice cream suppers with cake walks. Quilting bees would always bring a crown. Usually everyone would bring a covered dish for a luncheon.

One thing Rheatown never had was a saloon, although one had been planned. One of the early settlers, a Mr. Likens, made arrangements to open a saloon in a little log house. This was fifteen or twenty years before the Civil War outbreak. Someone buried a keg of powder in the chimney; it exploded. Mr. Likens received a broken leg and his would-be saloon was a complete wreck.

The caves in Rheatown drew many people in years past. One was known as the Bell Cave. Overhead at the entrance of the cave is a rock formation of a bell, which at one time had a complete clapper.

In 1872 John Robinson's Circus came to town. It was told that a boa constrictor of the South American variety escaped from its cage and took up its abode in the McCarty Mountains. A group of men armed themselves with suitable tools and went in search of it, but they came back empty handed. John Crawford was among those claiming to have seen it. He is reported to have seen it crossing the road near the William Davis home.

Another gruesome story was told of a panther being seen and heard in the area.

It was said to have screamed every night. For a long time people were afraid to leave their homes.

Besides Robinson's Circus, there was another circus that made annual showings. Tents were pitched on the vacant lot in front of the big spring. The officials stayed at the Keebler home.

Much excitement was created in the village at the appearance of the gypsies. One or two clans usually appeared annually. Sometimes they would stay a month and at other times only a short period. They usually pitched camp in a wooded area beyond the Bill Smith house on the old stage road. Their gala dress and fancy covered wagons always presented a carnival-like atmosphere. The younger set always wanted their fortunes told while the gypsies were in town.

BELL CAVE *The Bell Cave near Rheatown is very unique. It gets its name from a stalagmite formation on the ceiling of one of the rooms. This formation resembles a bell. Years ago the clapper was broken out by someone for a souvenir. Rheatown Creek runs through part of this cave, staying underground about a quarter of a mile.*

Music was a popular recreation for all ages. Everyone would gather in the parlor of a home that had a pump organ or a piano; some would bring string instruments. Emma Dukes was a noted pianist, as was Mary Donnelly. The Grant band, composed of Dave, Campbell, and Bill, furnished string music at many of these gatherings on winter evenings. In later years they were accompanied on the piano or organ by Dave's daughter, Ruth Grant Duncan. On these occasions everyone enjoyed singing or just listening to the music. Another musical invention that was enjoyed by those fortunate enough to own one was the gramophone. The large horned gramophone was the forerunner of the modern phonograph. Many of the homes had gramophones. Winter was the season for this recreation.

Games were enjoyed in that day when the work was all finished and the evening meal over. On cold winter nights the fun began.

Everyone gathered around the big table with a big fire blazing in the fireplace and played games. Fruit (apples and pears) stored in the cellar in the fall furnished refreshments each night. Popcorn was popped over the fire in the old-fashioned corn popper. Potatoes were baked in the ashes in the fireplace. Refreshments were seldom store-bought. Oranges and candy were a rare treat, usually enjoyed during the Christmas holidays. Long sticks of white chewing gum were a favorite of the children. The mothers made a delicious candy and popcorn balls, using molasses for special occasions.

The children and young people seemed to enjoy life in those bygone days. They enjoyed what they had and went on their merry way. On a hot summer day they would take a dip in the Rheatown Creek, where they had a swimming hole complete with plank diving board. If a boy was missing he could usually be found at the old swimming hole.

SHOUN SPRING *An interesting place, and one that was frequented by many people of Rheatown, was the Shoun Spring, located to the rear of Range's Store. Many a thirst has been quenched by walking across the green meadow to this spring. Tradition has it that if you drink from this spring you will always want to return.*

THE WILL RUPE HOUSE *The Will Rupe house is located on the west edge of Rheatown. The Rupe family lived here many years. A small branch runs in front and to the side of the house, making this a neat and cozy cottage. After the death of Mr. Rupe, the house was occupied by Charles and Effie Hankal and their son, Charles. Charles has lived there alone since the death of his parents.*

THE THOMAS BARN *This is one of the few old barns standing in Rheatown. It is built of rough sawed lumber and is well put together. This barn has been the scene of many a horse and mule-trading session, as well as cattle and hog trades by Buford and Reamer Thomas.*

BLACK PEOPLE
by
Sue R. Thomas

The history of Rheatown would not be complete without including the contribution of the black population to the community. They were all good citizens. Only a few were ex-slaves, and some were descendants of slaves. They were regarded as good workers. All of them owned their own homes. Some were more prosperous than others, and most of them provided for their families from the small land acreage on which they lived. Others worked for the white residents to supplement their income.

One reason for the small Negro population was that few of the early pioneers were financially able to purchase them. Another reason was that several of the pioneers were Quakers, or Friends as they were sometimes called, and were abolitionists, being opposed to slavery.

Two of the largest pioneer slave owners were Joseph and Nicholas Earnest. The former owned a number of slaves. Until a few years ago, some of the slave quarters still stood at the rear of the large brick home he erected in the eastern end of town. The front portion of the brick home is still in use and is owned by Mr. and Mrs. Edward Lamons. For a number of years the slave quarters were used for storage purposes. Frank Willis, a former slave, lived with the Earnest family a long time after the close of the Civil War. He had a son-in-law named Samp Ninney. "Aunt Hester", another slave of Henry Earnest and his wife, was known as a very fine cook.

For some reason, the older Negro residents were called uncle and aunt by the white residents.

Probably two of the best known and highly respected black residents were "Uncle King" and "Aunt Amelia Alexander". "Aunt Amelia" was better known as "Aunt Mealey". She belonged to Nicholas Earnest, and was only a small girl when the

Alexander House

Civil War ended. Not only was she a good cook, she served the community as a midwife for years. She was a small girl when the first train ran from Bristol to Knoxville. Her master brought all the slaves he owned to Chuckey to see the train pass through. She said it nearly scared the life out of her. The Earnest family taught all their slaves to read and write. Since the Negroes had no church at that time, Mr. Earnest took his slaves with his family to the Presbyterian Church in Rheatown. The Alexanders had one daughter who, when she was old enough, went to Greeneville as a maid for the Brown family. They also had a grandson, Alford, whom they reared. "Aunt Mealey" had to take him with her when she worked in the homes of the white people. After the Negroes had a school and church erected between Rheatown and Chuckey, she served as Sunday School Superintendent until her death. She was well versed in the Bible.

Another good Negro couple was Hardin Gillespie and his wife, "Aunt Bet". Hardin served in the Federal Army and died several years before "Aunt Bet". She lived alone in her small home surrounded by flowers, which she loved. She worked some for the white people and drew Hardin's pension when he died. "Aunt Bet" prided herself on her excellent health, with exception of a knee injury which she received when she stepped off a train before it stopped. She was returning from a trip to Knoxville. She had perfect teeth. When asked one time who made her teeth, she replied, "God Almighty". She attributed her good teeth to the fact that she kept them clean with sprigs from an althea bush. She once resided in a house not far from the Masonic Academy. She sold it to Elmer Barnes and purchased a little house and lot not far from the present United Methodist Church.

Gillespie House

Another black man, Wash Broyles, lived near the Masonic Academy. He had a large family of boys, Jim, Bob, John, and Dan. Wash worked for the late Nick P. Earnest for years.

Washington Greenlee and wife Rachel migrated from Virginia to Rheatown. As a former slave, he often told that his master took him to Yorktown when he was a little boy to see Lord Cornwallis surrender the Bristish Army to General George Washington. He lived to be 107 years of age.

"Aunt Minervah" lived in the last of the shacks built for students to attend Masonic Academy. Her mind was bad, and she lived to be very old. She had no family and no means of support, except what Rheatown residents gave her. She usually visited the Donnelly, Keebler, and Piper homes weekly, returning home with sufficient food to do her until her next visit to their homes. When she became unable to make the visits, persons from the above homes took baskets of food to her, and she was always remembered at Christmas time.

Andy Marvel, a good black man, lived on a hill between the main part of Rheatown and the Doyle farms. He stayed close to his little house, tended his garden, and raised chickens. He also raised his own meat. He sold chickens and eggs to buy his staple groceries. He was referred to as the weather prophet. Whenever it came a dry spell, people would contact him to find out when it might rain. His answer was always, "Not until it thunders."

"Aunt Hester Allison" lived to be quite old. She owned her home, which has

Allison Cabin

—51—

since been demolished. It stood back from the main street and was located about the third house on the east side of the road leading to the cemetery.

Russ Good was one black man who lived wherever he threw his hat. He worked for the Piper family for several years, doing odd turns when needed. In 1905, when William F. Piper established **The Rural Searchlight**, a weekly paper printed on a hand-turned press, Russ usually turned the press.

Jim Laughlin lived for many years in his little home across the road from the old Moody place. The road led from the center of Rheatown to the Quaker Knob and Pleasant Vale areas. When the highway was built through Rheatown, Bill Price was a member of the road crew. He met and married Etta. Etta and Bill's wedding occurred on a Sunday afternoon in front of Magistrate James R. White's home. It was well attended by the white people. They raised their family in the Laughlin house, which is now occupied by Ed Doyle. Bill worked for several of the white people, especially the Thomas and Range families. After Etta's death, the children moved away and Bill went to Greeneville and worked for the V.F.W. for several years before his death.

Noah Bradson was probably a slave of one of the Bradson families. He built a little house on one of the knolls in the Quaker Knob area. It was called, "Noah's Ark".

In 1875 Jacob Campbell came to Rheatown. His wife's name was Matilda. It is believed that she was a Bradson. They had several boys; among them were Bob, Lee, and Hugh. They built a little house in the valley between two large hills.

JUDD BOLINGER

The small Negro school between Rheatown and Chuckey was the only place of learning for the blacks in that area. The white students would come from Chuckey school at about the same time the Negro students would be going to Chuckey, and many times it would be an occasion for minor fights — for what reason, I never knew. Many a Negro child learned to read and write in this building.

Bill Price House

On one of these hills was found an Indian cemetery. The Campbells were hard working people. They had a good orchard of apples and peaches, and also raised strawberries.

Jim Russell, a fine looking Mulatto Negro, came to Rheatown as a young man and purchased a tanyard from Ham Shoun. The tanyard was located in the center of town and was in continuous operation for more than one hundred years. Jim was very successful in the business and was considered to be one of the wealthiest men in the village. He married Ann Steward, a beautiful Mulatto. They had no children but they raised a black boy, Stuart Miller. Stewart married a pretty Mulatto girl from Johnson City. At the time of Jim's death, he and Stewart and his family lived in the old Hiram Fraker home, now owned by Eula and Daryl Collete. The family moved to Jonesborough and later to Johnson City. Stewart died in Johnson City and his widow now lives in Boston, Massachusetts. They had several children. A small child of theirs is buried in Rheatown Cemetery, where most of the old black population is buried.

There are no black people residing in Rheatown at the present time.

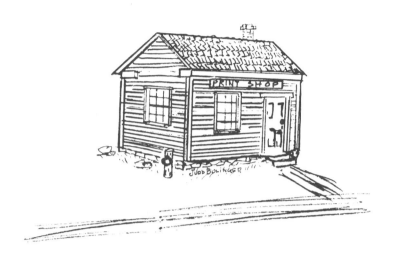

NEWSPAPER — THE RURAL SEARCHLIGHT *Another institution usually found only in the larger and more promising towns was the press. William F. Piper owned and edited* The Rural Searchlight. *This operation started in 1905. The newspaper was published weekly on a hand-turned press. Jim Tame of Afton and Russ Good, a black man, turned the press for ten cents an hour. Later Mr. Piper moved the press to Greeneville, where Charlie McInturff became a partner and eventually bought full rights to the paper.*

Mr. Piper returned to Rheatown and taught school there for two years before he returned to his printing career.

THE BEN BALES HOUSE *Located about one mile east of Rheatown, this house has horizontal siding and fancy trim, an example of the workmanship of the period when it was built. The house is now occupied by Alta Davis.*

DR. W. E. FRAKER HOUSE *Built sometime between 1875 and 1880, the bricks were burned one summer, the woodwork done one summer, and the inside finished the third summer.*

THE WILL DUKES HOUSE *Will Dukes, a leather worker, lived here. He later moved his family to Rogersville. Henrietta Bolinger and her daughter, Annie, lived here several years. The Rheatown Cemetery can be seen in the background.*

THE MOODY HOUSE *This modest house on the hill north of town was first owned by Harlan M. Moody and family. It was later occupied by Margaret and her son, Randall Moody. When Randall was a young man, he went to Knoxville to obtain employment. When he took his mother to Knoxville to live, he sold the home to W.D. "Bill" McCurry. It was later purchased by W.A. Bolinger and has been remodeled and made larger. Mrs. W.A. (Flora) Bolinger and son, Henry, now live here.*

THE LITTLE BRICK *This house is known as The "Little Brick". It gets its name from the fact that about one-half of the exterior is brick and the other half is verticle boards. It is built on two levels, the kitchen and dining room lower than the front portion of the house. This house is now owned by Bo Cooley.*

RHEATOWN CEMETERY
by
J. Allen Bolinger

It is doubtful if anyone living knows exactly when Rheatown Cemetery was first started. The most likely story states that sometime in the late 1700's there was a church somewhere in the vicinity of the present cemetery, possibly a Methodist church. In those days, as with a lot of churches of the present time, a cemetery was laid out as part of the church property; and the families would choose as many graves as needed there by forming a burial plot.

This church near Rheatown Cemetery possibly was a structure made of hand-made brick. As late as the 1940's hand-made bricks were used as head and foot markers for many graves. Even today a brick marker can be found here and there. Of course, the identity of the person has long been illegible.

Another traditional story tells that some of the very first graves were those of Revolutionary War soldiers. Years ago, before the dates on some of the monuments had frozen and chipped off, the dates went well back into the 1700's. The oldest legible marker that I have been able to find recently (in 1976) is a child's grave with the birth date of 1810 and the death date of 1811. This is a limestone marker and a few years will erode it beyond identity.

There is a large area in the west center of the cemetery which may contain the graves of many Civil War soldiers killed in the battle of Rheatown, which took place near—if not on—the site of the cemetery. If there are graves in this area they are all unmarked.

The cemetery has been increased in size at least twice. Once around 1920 the Fisher family and the Will Church family gave a strip of land off their farms to the cemetery. This strip on the east side was some thirty feet wide and over two hundred feet long. Just recently (1975) a small triangular plot known as the Frank Fisher plot was given to the Rheatown Cemetery Association by Mrs. Frank Fisher.

By the orderly laying out of the available space in the cemetery there are about one hundred and thirty grave plots available through the association. The funds raised in this manner go into the trust fund for the upkeep of the cemetery.

There is someone who always takes a special interest in every community project, and Mrs. J. Newt (Clara) Range was such a person. For years she took an interest in the Rheatown Cemetery and worked many hours there to keep it looking nice. But the time came that she could no longer work there; however, her interest in this project never failed during her lifetime.

To create interest in the cemetery, Mrs. Range was successful in forming a board of trustees. Members of this board were Jimmie Rodgers, Sam Range, and J. Allen Bolinger. This informal group was instrumental in making several improvements in the cemetery, such as getting the road widened, building some much-needed fences, and painting and repairing existing fences. Sam Range secured an ET&WNC truck body to be used for a tool house. At this time the cemetery began to be mowed on a regular basis as money became available.

The devotion and interest of people like Mrs. Range is what prompted a group of people to begin talking about forming a cemetery association.

After the death of Mrs. Franke White Denney in 1968, the James R. White family gave a memorial gift to the cemetery. This gift was placed in Home Federal Savings and Loan Association with the interest to be used for the upkeep of the cemetery. When J. Earl Thomas died the same year his sons, George and Norman, also made a memorial gift to the fund.

With this fund in Home Federal Savings and Loan, an organizational meeting was called on April 29, 1971, at the Rheatown Methodist Church for the purpose of establishing an organization to raise money for a trust fund, using the interest to maintain the cemetery.

The first president to be elected was Bobby Weems of Chuckey. His vice president was Harold Campbell, also of Chuckey. Mrs. Dale (Edith) Jaynes was elected secretary and is still serving in that capacity. O.L. "Jack" McCurry was elected treasurer. A three-member trustee board was elected, with one trustee to be elected each year and one to go off the board each year. The first trustee members were James Winslow, three years; J. Allen Bolinger, two years; and Mrs. Jack (Helen) McCurry, one year.

A set of by-laws was drafted by the organization with the understanding that they could be amended or added to as circumstances warranted. The organization was to be non-profit, and possibly would take out a charter of incorporation; but this has not been done at this writing.

The organization is required to have at least one meeting a year in May to elect officers, transact business, hear reports, and make plans for the year.

The first president, Bobby Weems, served two terms; and J. Allen Bolinger is now serving his third term as president.

By letting interested families know about the organization and our needs to set up a trust fund, we were able to raise a sizeable amount. The interest from the fund and money given us directly for the upkeep each year has made it possible to keep the cemetery in good condition the year round. Mrs. J. Newt (Clara) Range not only worked hard in the cemetery for years, but also made a substantial provision in her will to be added to the trust fund.

All has not been pleasant. This summer (1976) someone broke the lock on the tool shed and stole some of the tools, including two good lawn mowers—one purchased in the spring and used very little. It takes a low-class thief to steal from a cemetery.

I have observed the cemetery closely for several years doing work as I had time, especially when my brother, Billie Bolinger, was sick. I would come to visit him and spend some time working at the cemetery.

Once when Mrs. Range and I were visiting the cemetery, she made a statement of which I am truly appreciative: "This ground is sacred to me. When you have so many loved ones and friends buried in a cemetery it takes on an air of sacredness."

It is a great reassurance to me and others to know that steps have been taken to perpetuate the care of the Rheatown Cemetery. I remember when my father, Henry V. Bolinger, was buried in May 1921, most of the cemetery was unkept and untidy. It was overgrown with honeysuckle, sassafras and locust. Some of the plots were as well kept as they are today. My mother, Cordie Bolinger, and Aunt Ann Bolinger saw that our plot was kept clean; of course, Billie and I did a lot of the work. Other plots were kept neat too: Marshalls, Frakers, Morleys, Collettes, Keeblers, Ranges, Thomases, Rodgers, Winslows, Whites, and others.

The black people did a good job keeping their portion of the cemetery clean. Such old timers as Abner Johnson, King Alexander, Bill Price, and Lee and Hugh Campbell especially worked hard on their family plots. Many people also remember that Bill Price laid off the graves in the cemetery for many years.

I think it proper that special recognition be given to some people who have given generously of their time and efforts toward the upgrading of the cemetery. They are Mrs. Jack (Helen) McCurry, who has been in charge of maintenance since her husband O.L. "Jack" McCurry became ill. However he remained local treasurer until his death, April 15, 1976. To Mr. James Winslow for his efficient handling of the finances; also Steve Finkle, who has done an excellent job of maintenance.

I am glad that I had a part, however small, in the upgrading, both with physical labor and financial gifts, of this resting place of so many fine friends and loved ones.

The Annual Decoration is held the fourth Sunday in May. Friends and loved ones from far and near gather for the occasion to honor the memory of dear ones who rest in the Rheatown Cemetery.

As I was sitting on the old church bench at the cemetery one spring day in May 1976, my thoughts turned to the bicentennial year of the nation. A breeze was blowing as I noticed a small American flag being blown against the marble stone of a Civil War veteran. As the stars and stripes of this soft cotton flag gently caressed the stone, I imagined I could hear it say, "Sleep on, brave soldier, and have no fear. I will watch over your resting place until I am tattered and worn; and then I will be replaced by a new one, as you were replaced in the line of battle by a fresh young soldier. Dear fallen one, your devotion makes it possible for me to still wave over the land of the free and the home of the brave."

On decoration day, flags are placed on the graves of the soldiers who have stones to identify their resting places.

Each spring and summer, many out of town visitors stop by the cemetery to visit graves of their friends and loved ones. They pause to rest in the shade of the stately cedar trees which are among the oldest in the state of Tennessee.

THE ARGENBRIGHT HOUSE *Mrs. Argenbright and her daughter, Cleo, lived in this house on the Old Stage Road west of Rheatown many years. This sturdy house is still standing and is occupied by the Raymond Estepp family.*

ERRATA

PAGE 61
>BYERLY (Insert after BRYANT)
>John W., 5-27-1834, 12-28-1863

PAGE 63
>GILLESPIE
>Wife Bett, died 9-17-1924

>GODSEY
>Vivian, 1927-1982
>Wife of Earl Jr.

>GUIRE
>Bessie Moyer 4-18-1890, 3-22-1993
>Wife of Frank

>McCURRY
>Helen Thomas, 12-9-1909, 5-25-1981
>(Wife of O.L. "Jack")
>(Daughter of William Earle & Lulu)

>MORLEY (not MORELY)

PAGE 64
>PAINTER
>J.H., 1841, 5-9-1927

>PRICE
>Bloxie (Wife of James)
>Emma Mae, 1913, 1966

>RANGE
>John Newton, 12-8-1874, 11-11-1950
>Wife, Clara Winslow, 11-21-1880
>9-6-1971 (Sister of W. Clay Winslow)

>SAMPSON
>Wm. Ward, Civil War
>Wife, Hariett Melissa, 5-27-1927

>SYERLY - Should be BYERLY
>(See correction for page 61)

PAGE 65
>In last line under Thomas should be
>Guy Peyton not Paton

>NO TOMBSTONES
>BALES
>Mrs. B.F., died 7-26-1918
>Should be FRAKER not FRAHER
>Should be RUPE not REYRE

Copied from Tombstones in Cemetery

ADAMS
J.C., 6-23-1844, 4-19-1868
 (Co. B 11th Tennessee Inf.)

ALEXANDER
King, 1842, 1915

ALLEN
Harvey D., 1-18-1831, 5-29-1885
 Wife, Martha O., 9-18-1831, 5-17-1890
 Daughter, Sarah, 1866, 1884
 Son, James G., 5-9-1864, 9-13-1883
James, 6-14-1799, 7-18-1877
 Wife, Martha, 10-23-1803, 9-10-1862

ALLISON
Nancy, 8-2-1833, 11-28-1905

ANDERSON
Rev. W.R., 3-16-1891, 10-24-1963
 Wife, Lucy J., 4-28-1892, 5-21-1980

ARGENBRIGHT
Barbara Ann, 6-26-1841, 2-3-1899
Wm. H., 1-21-1843, 12-10-1905

BAKER
Jonathan (Co. G 4th Tennessee Cav.)

BARKLEY
William, 4-8-1785, 4-19-1850

BARNES
Mary Elizabetrh, 1946, 1948
Roy V., 4-20-1881, 4-6-1972
 Wife, Martha E. Swiney, 9-19-1892,
 2-22-1972

BICKNELL
Margaret, 2-24-1854, 11-25-1884

BOLINGER
Flora Mae, 1907-1990
 (Wife of William A.)
James Henry, 8-17-1927, 12-22-1988
 (Son of Flora Mae & Willie)
W.H., 6-14-1826, 2-2-1916
 Wife, Henrietta G., 5-13-1831, 2-2-1916
 Daughter, Annie, 10-5-1861, 3-30-1945
 Son, Henry V., 8-4-1871, 5-14-1921
 Wife, Cordelia L., 5-13-1874, 8-2-1947
 Infant twin daughters, 6-3-1913
 Son, William A., 1900-1973
 Son, Allen, 4-1-1929, 3-11-1951

BRANNO
Elizabeth Ann, 4-30-1841, 3-20-1859

(Wife of John A.)
Mary Ellen, 5-2-1839, 5-24-1860
 (Wife of Wm. F.)

BROWN
Miriam, 1841, 1909

BROYLES
Grace E., 1871, 1927
 (Wife of D.N.)

BRYANT
George E., 1861, 1941

CAMPBELL
Alice, 7-29-1854, 6-19-1899
 Wife of Charles
Arthur Lee, 1919, 1942
Fannie S., 7-14-1942, 9-10-1968
Harriett, M.J., 1849, 8-11-55
 (6 years, 1 month, 10 days)
Helen K., 1903 (Wife of James)
Hubert C., 10-30-1940, 1-20-1968
Hugh, 8-3-1893, 12-18-1956
 Wife, Leo E., 8-5-1896, 5-14-1961
Jacob, 8-1-1840, 1914
Jake, 10-21-1840, 3-28-1915
 Wife, Matilda, 4-14-1848, 8-26-1923
James, 1884, 1948
Jesse James, 10-15-1842, 1-15-1844
Lee H., 3-20-1893, 4-5-1959
 (Pfc. Tenn. 20 Engineers World War I)
Mary E., 1851, 7-13-1855
 (4 years, 2 months, 20 days)
Nancy Ann, 4-5-1810, 1-11-1844
Vada, 1900, 1978

CARDWELL
Ida F. Dukes, 8-30-1860, 9-4-1900
 (Wife of G.A.)
 Son, Jerome, 1891, 1891

CHADESTER
Margaret, 1851, 1852

CHURCH
Joel, 4-18-1845, 2-21-1919
 Wife, Ada Jane, 12-12-1849, 1-12-1899
 Son, Bijah
William Martin, 2-6-1867, 7-5-1928
 Wife, Eliza Jane, 5-16-1863, 9-18-1918

COLLETTE
Charlie, 12-27-1872, 1-1-1954
 Wife, Maggie Keller, 4-18-1878,
 3-16-1910

Son, Frank, 1905, 1910
Otta B., 1916, 1917
  (Son of Sam & Letha)
Samuel William, 6-21-1883, 3-10-1932
Sophronia, 4-6-1865, 9-29-1928

COLLINS
Barbara J., 2-9-1937, 2-9-1937
Jessie, 1877, 1878
  (daughter of Johnathan and Syntha)
Lydia, 2-13-__, 10-2-__
S., 8-9-1804, 6-10-1861

CONN
James K., 8-10-1844, 1-29-1915
John, 5-26-1811, 1-6-1886
Nancy, 4-2-1820, 7-23-1866
P.F., 9-21-1849, 7-5-1919
Wife, N.J., 12-10-1847, 3-10-1880
Robert L., 1878, 1880
Stepp, 1859, 1873

CORBY
Herman C., 1-22-1883
Wife, Laura Church, 12-13-1874
  6-25-1948

CRAWFORD
John, 1809, 1893
Wife, Elizabeth, 9-30-1811, 4-23-1872

CULFORD
John, 1848, 1895
Wife, Mary Conn Scott, 10-2-1847,
  5-4-1900

DEBUSK
Isaac, 1-24-1794, 6-10-1879
Wife, Mary Jane, 9-25-1804, 8-5-1887
Daughter, Rachel, 11-29-1840,
  5-10-1883

DOBBINS
Edith, 1901, 1903
  (Daughter of S. & V.)

DONNELLY
Robert H.M., 1-2-1835, 3-3-1927
  (1st Lt., Capt., Maj. 13th Reg. Tennessee
  Vol. Cal. USA 1863-1865)
Wife, Eliza J., 7-1-1840, 6-23-1906
Daughter, Onnie Theo, 1882, 1907
Son, Cecil Blain, 8-30-1886, 8-26-1922
Daughter, Caroline, 1864, 1948
Daughter, Mary, 1877, 1966
Son, John, 1871, 1949
Daughter, Etta E., 1867, 1868
Daughter, Margaret C., 1872, 1872

DOTSON
Albert B., 4-16-1880, 2-7-1927
Wife, Minnie Bell, 12-15-1888, 3-6-1968
Son, Carl Rueben, 11-19-1908,
  8-19-1968

DOYLE
Eddie Lee, 1963-1991
  (Son of Mary E. & Ed)

DUKES
_____, 7-20-1835, 11-__-1886
Gracie, 1896, 1898
Homer L., 1888, 1898
Jane, 1804, 1-12-1866
  (Wife of James, age 62)
Sarah E., 4-10-1837, 7-9-1888
Winnie F., 1901, 1902

DYER
Walter E., 1892, 1942
Son, Walter R., 1919, 1922

EARNEST
Timanda, 10-25-1827, 3-18-1910

ELLIOTT
Charles, 1860, 1861
  (Son of John)

FRAKER
H.D., 8-4-1826, 2-27-1911
Wife, Sarah E., 1-9-1826, 9-19-1910
Son, Dr. W.E., 2-5-1851, 8-29-1908
Wife, Emma Morley, 4-8-1854,
  1-5-1939 (daughter of Dr. J.R. &
  Rachel)

FRENCH
Joseph, 3-28-1877, 9-5-1905

FISHER
Bessie, 3-22-1888, 11-16-1907
David Elmo, 1871, 1877
David N., 1866, 1868
Rev. James G., 12-13-1847, 8-17-1908
Wife, Mary Elizabeth, 12-11-1857
  10-29-1914
John Edwards, 1872, 1873
John Henry, 4-16-1854, 5-23-1923
Wife, Lydia Day, 10-31-1859,
  12-15-1935
Mary Dukes, 3-28-1851, 5-31-1886
  (Wife of Lewis - Daughter of William)

GAMMONS
Infant of J.G. & E.A., 1-18-1848

GILLESPIE

Harden, 1-4-1831, 11-29-1909
  Wife, Bett, died in the late 1920's

GODSEY
Earl, 1895, 1965
  Wife, Hattie, 1896
Vivian, 1927-1982

GOOD
Martha Milburn, 2-26-1834, 1-25-1894
  (Wife of Hartsell, killed in war, buried
  National Cemetery #4881 Nashville,
  Tennessee, 7-27-1831, 7-14-1868)

GRAY
George W., 1-22-1823, 4-19-1897
  Wife, Mary J., 11-8-1830, 3-30-1910
Roxanner A., 11-26-1852, 1-26-1871

GREENE
John David, 8-27-1953, 6-4-1993

HENRY
Mary Lou, 1923-1980
  (Daughter of Ollie)
Ollie Fisher, 1887, 1975

HUFF
Wade, 1904, 1960

HUNDLEY
Mary, 1795, 3-21-1857
  (Wife of John S. - age 62)

JACKSON
Helen Barnes, 1909-1993
  (Wife of Otis)
Otis, 1909, 1957
  Son, Virgil S., 1940, 1940

JOHNSON
Larry, 1950, 1950
Thomas, 1-13-1804, 4-17-1870
  Wife, Mahala, 9-11-1806, 7-16-1899
Wm. P., 10-17-1838, 3-2-1917
  Wife, Addie R., 2-17-1857, 3-21-1911
  Son, James K., 1893, 1894

KEEBLER
J.D., 3-7-1847, 11-28-1938
  Wife, Sarah Piper, 7-22-1852, 8-26-1934
  Son, James G., 2-23-1876, 2-19-1921
    Wife, Minnie White, 6-7-1878,
    10-9-1971

KICHLOE
Florence, 1881, 1957

MARSHALL
Rev. Eli, 7-18-1833, 9-23-1909
  Wife, Julia S., 7-27-1855, 5-19-1925

Irene May, 1894, 1894
  (Daughter of Joe)

McADAMS
Robert N., 1847, 1921
  Wife, Mary Margaret, 1854, 1946
  Daughter, Bessie, 1878, 1947
  Son, Hugh I., 1884, 1921
Thomas C., 1855, 1920

McCURRY
Helen Thomas, 12-9-1909, 5-25-1981
  (Wife of O.L. "Jack")
  (Daughter of William Earls & Lulu
  White Thomas)
Mary Emily Dukes, 1-12-1824, 5-25-1855
  (Wife of James)
O.L. "Jack", 1-16-1909, 4-15-1976
  Son, William Earl, 1933, 1933

McKEEHAN
Carolina, 7-29-1833, 6-2-1872
J.H., no dates
  (Co. A, 3rd Pa. W.F.)
John C., 4-21-1823, 7-9-1896
Nannie M., 6-3-1829, 9-21-1878
Wm. A., 7-14-1832, 10-26-1896

METTETOL
Alexis, age 1, 4-14-1884

MILLER
James W., 1912, 1912

MOODY
Elizabeth, 1844, 1916
  Daughter, Margaret, 1878, 1932
Harland M., 12-23-1831, 3-22-1870

MORELY
Dr. J.R., 8-17-1830, 8-19-1907
  Wife, Rachel R. Donnelly, 5-21-1832
  6-16-1913
  Daughter, Elizabeth, 1856, 1856
  Daughter, Cary, 1856, 1856

MOYERS
Johnathan, 9-18-1850, 3-19-1884
Johnny
Lizzie, 1-20-1852, 5-16-1931
Norad, 3-20-1888, 9-18-1912
Robbie
Rome M., 5-30-1885, 10-30-1962
Sarah
William

NASH
Bascom, 1945, 1945

PAINTER

J.H., 1841, no death date
Wife, Rosanah, 1843, 1912

PATRICK
Jennie, 1960, 1960

PIPER
Albert M., 8-20-1820, 6-11-1873
Wife, Martha O., 12-19-1824, 5-14-1869

PRICE
Barbie??? (Wife of James)
Emma Mae, 9-13-1996
(Daughter of Bill & Etta)
Floyd (Son of Bill & Etta)
William M., 3-8-1877, 6-10-1968
Wife, Etta, 1892, 1943
Son, Clarence, 1910, 1920
Daughter, Mary, 1910, 1957

RADISONE
Angelo Gierra, 2-29-1920, 7-17-1990

RANGE
Cleo Huffman, 1900-1989
(Wife of Sam)
John Newton, 12-8-1874, 11-11-1950
Wife, Clara Winslow, 11-21-1880,
9-6-1971 (Sister of W. Clay)
Son, Samuel N., 10-6-1906, 6-29-1969

RAWLES
Ellen, 3-29-1861, 6-20-1891
(Wife of C.M.)

RESER
C.
Charlie B., 12-18-1869, 2-12--1890
Emma N., 1884
Malinda A., 1845, 2-18-1877
Sarah M. 8-29-1842, 2-18-1877
W.F.
Willie, 1874, 1876

RHEA
Maggie, 1-25-1861, 8-10-1886
(Wife of J.S. - the man that gave
Rheatown its name)

RICHARDSON
John H., 4-2-1892, 3-2-1961
Lily Dale, 11-19-1897, 10-3-1971
William Melton, 1855, 1900
Wife, Rebecca Isabelle, 1857, 1936
Willie, 1899-1983

RODGERS
Rev. Henderson F., 1871, 1947
Wife, Ella D., 5-16-1868, 4-27-1906
Daughter, Mary, 1905, 1906

Daughter, Glenna, 1-1-1897, 10-20-1917
2nd wife Laura, 1880, 1950
Son, James D., 12-6-1908, 5-15-1971

RUPE
Ellie E., 1879, 1880
(daughter of A.W. & Mary A.)

RUSSELL
Anna B., 7-12-1853, 7-16-1912
J.R., 1852, 1919

SAMPSON
Wm. Ward, Civil War
Wife, Harriett Melissa

SCOTT
John Gilliam, 1848, 1895
(Wife, Mary E. Conn - see Culford)
William C., 8-17-1847, 3-17-1915
Wife, Lydia E., 10-4-1847, 4-18-1915
Infant son

SHOUN
E. Clay, 4-5-1854, 4-7-1888
Wife, Lizzie T. Morley, 11-12-1858,
1-3-1894
Son, Infant, 1886, 1886
Son, Tullie M., 1883, 1947
Son, Roe D., 1887, 1955

SMITH
Lucindia Moyer, 10-14-1852, 6-27-1908
William L., 12-10-1861, 2-10-1940

SQUIBB
Georgia R., 1870, 1871
Nellie O., 1875, 1898
Tommie, 1868, 1884

STARR
James, 5-10-1797, 8-30-1875

SWINEY
Ada M., 1894, 1940
Aldon, 1915, 1917
Beatrice, 1917, 1923
Hobert, 1930, 1930
James B., 1921, 1921
James I. 12-31-1868, 7-28-1900
L. Edgar, 1890, 1947
Minnie E., 1875, 1924

SYERLY
John W., 5-29-1834, 12-23-1863

TESTERMAN
Cordia B., 1927, 1927
George, 1931, 1931
Hubert R., 1926, 1926

Patsy, 1934, 1934

THOMAS
Albert B., 10-23-1914, 4-14-1980
Duncan Reesen, 7-21-1848, 7-30-1897
  Wife, Mattie Baxter Reams, 10-18-1857,
    3-29-1944
  Son, William Earle, 7-16-1884,
    11-11-1925
    Wife, Lulu White, 9-7-1887, 2-11-1971
    Son, Duncan Reamer, 2-4-1906,
      11-24-1942
    Son, Niles Franklin "Jack", 7-22-1921,
      1-23-1953 (Pfc. U.S. Army
      World War II)
    Son, James Earl, 2-29-1908, 10-9-1968
    Son, Guy Paton, 8-9-1914, 10-18-1971

WHITE
Elizabeth J. Morely, 3-2-1824, 8-10-1884
  Son, Charles B., 12-23-1849, 8-19-1893
  Son, James Randolph, 3-12-1852,
    9-4-1935
    Wife, Mary Emily Good, 1-15-1859,
      4-15-1926 (Daughter of Hartsell &
      Martha Milburn Good)
    Son, Walter, 1880, 1880
    Daughter, Elma, 1896, 1896
    Son, Elbert Carl, 1896, 1915
    Son, James Henry, 10-9-1892,
      10-10-1918 (Member of Co G, 327th
      U.S. Inf. 82nd Division Chaleau
      Thierry, France) World War I
Infant White
Jack, 1862, 1907
  Wife, Myrtle, 1869, 1958
  Son, Karl V., 7-19-1891, 4-5-1912
    Wife, Franke White Denney,
      4-29-1890, 1-16-1968
      Infant twins of Karl V. and Franke
William Carl, 11-26-1921
  (Infant son of Mr. and Mrs. I.W. White)

WILSON
Amelia A., 12-1-1852, 3-2-1919
  (Wife of Hardin)
G. Randolph, 1878, 1896
Joseph B., 5-8-1846, 7-9-1921
Margaret Ann, 1-15-1834, 11-10-1908

WINSLOW
Addie, 1885, 1905
Robert B., 2-9-1815, 11-18-1884
  Wife, Mary M., 1-29-1814, 12-15-1883
Ruth, 1926, 1926
Samuel B., 10-8-1841, 6-18-1905
  Wife, Fannie P., 2-14-1847, 12-17-1922

W. Clay, 1878, 1965
  Wife, Sarah, 1889, 1929
Walter, 1906, 1911

YAKLEY
Mary E., 10-8-1856, 6-19-1928
  Daughter, Martha, 1891, 1892
W.H., 1884, 1959

YOUNG
Annie L. Fisher, 10-26-1887, 5-6-1915

NO TOMBSTONES

ALEXANDER
Mrs. _____, died 12-9-23

BALES
Mrs. B.F., died 7-26-1918

BARKLEY
Eula L., 7-30-1931

BOND
Martha B., died 2-11-1940

CAMPBELL
Arthur Lee, died 11-25-1942

FRAHER
_____, died 6-20-1920
Child, died 1-8-1923

GRUGER
Infant, died 10-15-1926
JOHNSON
Mattie, died 7-9-27

LEWIS
Mrs. L.J., died 9-10-1919

MOODY
Child, died 1-8-1920

PATRICK
Mrs. _____, died 11-6-1917

PETER
Child, died 8-15-1918
  (Son of J.D. Peter)

REYRE
Mary A., died 10-5-1911
  (Wife of H.A.)

WILLIS
Infant, died 10-23-1925
  (Son of Ted)

YAHLEY
John, died 6-4-1938

McKEEHAN HOUSE *This house had a stone foundation and was framed with hewn timber. Other owners were Major William C. Scott, Jim Russell, Earle Thomas and Henry V. Bolinger. This sturdy house was owned by Mrs. Earle (Lulu) Thomas when it was destroyed by fire in 1934.*

THE MARION CLOYD HOUSE *Marion and Nora Cloyd and their daughter, Lucy, lived in this modest and comfortable home in the upper east end of Rheatown. It was later owned by Charles Collette.*

THE QUAKERS
by
Sue Piper Thomas

In 1770, a great influx of Quakers, known as the Religious Society of Friends, came to this area. A large number of them were from North Carolina, and some from Pennsylvania and Virginia. They settled at the headwaters of Little Limestone. For some reason they moved farther down and settled in and around Rheatown. Several settled on the north side of McCarty's Mountain, now referred to as the Quaker Knobs.

The late Capt. Joe J. Marshall of Limestone was an authority on this religious organization. His ancestors were Quaker ministers. His father was the Rev. Eli Marshall, and his great-grandfather was the Rev. Abraham Marshall. The ancestral home of the Marshalls was in the west end of Rheatown.

Among the early Quaker pioneers were William Reece, Garrett and Peter Dillion, William and Abraham Smith, Solomon David, John B. Bales, Samuel and Mordicai Ellis, Abraham Marshall, Samuel Pearson, Samuel Stanfield, and George Hayworth.

They built what is known as the New Hope Meeting House. For about one hundred years the church annals were dominated by such names as Marshall, Ellis, Bales, Pickering, Horner, and many others.

Ancestors of the late Congressman B. Carroll Reece and U.S. Senator James B. Frazier worshipped in the meeting house.

Samuel Frazier purchased a one hundred acre tract of land in the Sinking Creek area, now known as the Quaker Knobs. It was granted to him for the sum of twelve dollars and fifty cents and signed by Alexander Martin, governor of North Carolina, at Newbern on November 27, 1792. Frazier deeded a little over three acres of the land for the New Hope Meeting House and cemetery. This was after the church was built. He was paid three pounds and ten shillings in English money.

The first building was a log structure. Later a brick building was erected. A school house was also built on the property. The church served the community from 1795 until 1886, when the big snow came and caved in the roof and ruined the edifice. After that, the school building was used for services.

Of these meetings, the late Capt. J.J. Marshall said, "In my mind's eye I can see John Bales, the ruling elder, sit down at the head of the meeting in silence and wait on the Lord and maybe for a whole hour you could not hear a sound."

In 1867, John Hoover, a relative of the late President Hoover and an elder in the Quaker Church in Iowa, arrived at the Quaker Knobs to help it recover from the disruption resulting from the Civil War. He restarted and maintained the school. He remained there until 1879 when Mr. and Mrs. John M. Minton, uncle and aunt of Ex-president Hoover, took over the teaching duties.

Among those attending the school from Rheatown was Mary Good, who later married James R. White. At that time she resided on the site of the present Willard Jeffers home.

Some noted men visited the New Hope Meeting House. Among them were Bevin Braithwait, prime minister of England under some part of Queen Victoria's reign,

and his secretary and personal attendant, Dr. John Thomas of London.

The second Sunday in November was set for annual meetings. People came from far and near to attend. They filled the church and school to overflowing. Hundreds had to stand on the outside where fires were built to keep them warm. Preaching was also held on the outside. At one meeting it was recorded that the church had a membership of over four hundred. It was a great spiritual event.

In 1815, a General Convention of Quakers was held in Greene County. John Marshall was the secretary of the meeting. Catherine Hammer, a noted Quaker minister, preached at the church at one time.

The Quakers of this area are of special historical interest because of their early leadership in the anti-slavery movement. The first anti-slavery newspaper in America, *The Emancipator*, was published in Jonesborough in 1820. It was dedicated to freeing the slaves.

The Quakers, long regarded as one of the most conscientious and sober-minded Christian sects, were noted for their quaint social customs, dress, and lack of ceremony. They set themselves apart by refusing to pay tithes, to take an oath, to bear arms, and refusing to doff their hats in the presence of what one might call their superiors. The women wore plain gray dresses and bonnets. The men wore broad brimmed hats. Their coats had no collars and their sleeves no buttons.

Of special interest was their mode of marriage. The usual procedure included an announcement of the couple's intention to unite. No ceremony by a minister was used. Only members present signed a document as witnesses.

In 1928, prayers of the Quakers were heard all the way to the White House. The late President Hoover sent a $25.00 check to help repair the church which had ceased to be used because of needed repairs.

For several years the New Hope Meeting House was badly in need of repairs. It has now been restored by the Heritage Trust and is one of the landmarks of Greene County. Blanche Pickering headed the restoration. Services are held once a month through the summer with good attendance. For the past two years a homecoming has been held on decoration day, the third Sunday in June. Restoration of this landmark was the first project of the Greene County Historical Society.

QUAKER FAMILIES

Maupin Family

Another-well known Quaker family, whose descendants still reside in the Rheatown area, near Pleasant Vale, was the Maupin family. The Maupins emigrated from France to escape religious persecution. They first settled in Friendsville, Tennessee, later moving into this area.

Albert B. Maupin and his wife, Hannah, were devout Quakers. Mrs. Maupin's sister, Margaret Bales Hackney, was a minister during 1915-1916.

Joseph (Joe) Maupin can recall when Calvin Jones, a noted Quaker minister, visited his parents' home. Joe's parents, Joseph Hoag Maupin and Elizabeth Streshley Maupin, opened their home to many traveling Quakers, and are still remembered for their hospitality to their visitors. Both Margaret B. Hackney and Rhoda Bales frequented the Maupin home. Joseph Bales was the cousin of Joseph Hoag Maupin.

Bales Family

One of the most notable Quaker ministers in the area was Rhoda Bales. She was a descendant of the Bales family that came to the Quaker Knobs in the late 1790's from England. Rhoda, along with her brothers, Dr. Tom Bales and William Penn Bales, was reared in the Quaker Knob community. She experienced a calling—''An inward light''—that led to many years of teaching, preaching, and helping people. Her ministry took her to various parts of the country, yet her work at the Knobs has been best remembered. One of her neighbors said of her, ''Her tenderness, kindness, loving smile, and a warm handclasp made her one of the most remembered Quakers ever to frequent the Knobs.''

It was her desire to be buried at the Quaker Knobs. She died on a cold November day in 1926 at the age of seventy. On the day she was buried, a close friend of hers said it was a shame the weather was so bad. Rhoda was so good it seemed the birds should be singing and the daffodils blooming all around. Her marker reads, "She Hath Done What She Could."

William Penn Bales returned to Rheatown in 1925. He lived on the present site of the Otterbein United Methodist Parsonage. His wife, Mary Ann Garner Bales, was also a Quaker minister. For several years she held services in the Quaker Knob church each Sunday afternoon.

ST. JOSEPH CHAPEL, CHUCKEY A.M.E. ZION CHURCH *This church is located between Chuckey and Rheatown. The black people from both communities attended this church.*

When the deed was written in 1898 the property was deeded to the church trustees. From Rheatown: Andy Marble, Jim Laughlin, Jim Russell, King Alexander and Butler Taylor. From Chuckey: Jake Campbell, John Earnest, Sam Miller, John Greeneway and Abner Johnson.

The church was dedicated in 1904 and has been well preserved.

In the early 1900's there was a school adjoining the church. Several years ago the children began to attend other schools and the building was demolished.

METHODISM IN RHEATOWN

The first record we have of a Methodist Church in Rheatown is 1844. Goodspeed, however, says that a Methodist church had been erected in the upper end of the village by 1820. This church could have been located near the Rheatown Cemetery.

In 1844 a Methodist congregation was organized in Rheatown. A log church was erected on the Stage Road in the east end of town on the Earnest farm, near the entrance to the Rheatown Cemetery.

We know this church existed because we have a copy of the deed and the first ledger dated the 8th of February 1844. All subscriptions and payments were recorded in this ledger by the secretary. A large portion of the ledger is not legible due to age, and the name of the secretary is unknown at this writing.

This is a partial list of the subscribers spelled as they were recorded in the ledger:

Rev. Wm. Eaken
Jess S. Reeves
Charles Collins
James Depew
Joseph H. Earnest
Wm. Barkley
John Y. Matthews
James Yelton
Hickles Earnest
Jesse Oliver
Jonathen Earven
Jacob Collette
Elias Remel
William Milburn
Wm. Bright
Lewis Grubbs
Cornel Earnest
A.G. Fellars
James Simpson

Shephard Ervin
Levi Hartman
Jonathan R. Collins
Uriah Collins
Peter Reese
David Marshall
Peter Collins
James Dukes
W.L. French
David Ripley
John Anderson
L.A. Cox
Jeremiah Rose
William Liebs
William Archer
John Pickering
Nathannel Thomson
John Fraker

The following people made payments in 1845:

John C. Cumberland
John Ranken
Adam Chashday
William Stanfield
David Reese
John Sneed
Elizabeth Roiston
William Hicks
David Reese
Thomas Ripley
James Hise

Jesse Wright
Joseph Shields
Matthew Campbell
Mehabe Ann Scott
Samuel Rhea
Harvey More
George Boise
T. Naff
W.E. Fraker
Margaret Ripley
Louis Launsford

Rev. John Y. Broiles	William Boise
James Johnston	C.A. Roiston
R.K. Marsh	Thomas Hunt
John Riddle	Joseph H. Gilman
G.M.D. Parr	Joseph Whinnery
James P. Chettister	

These payments were made by labor, lumber and small amounts of cash.

The parsonage for this church stood behind the old freight depot across the creek from the Rheatown United Methodist Church.

The first minister was the Rev. Wm. Eaken who was noted for his fiery sermons. The last remembered minister was John Hughes. Soon after the Civil War the church was closed, and several of the members moved their membership to the new Methodist Church in Chuckey.

Rheatown Methodist Episcopal Church South

Methodist Episcopal Church South

The citizens of Rheatown were about equally divided between the North and South after the Civil War.

Soon after the end of the war the church was organized by the southern sympathizers and by families who refused to move their membership to Chuckey after the Methodist Church closed.

The foundation of the church was of rock. The logs for the building were donated by Thomas Doyle. The men cut the logs from the Doyle Knob (part of McCarty's Mountain), and they were hauled to the saw mill by Mr. Doyle using four large oxen. His son, Oath, and the men from the village assisted him. The Doyle family was of Catholic faith but often attended the churches in the community.

The church was well built with six large windows with iridescent panes and two entrance doors. There were two aisles with long pews in the center and short ones on each side. The labor was donated, and most likely the church furniture was built by some of the local carpenters.

The flue was built near the center of the church. One large stove heated the building. The men and boys cut the wood, hauled it to the church, and built the fires for the services.

Light was furnished by kerosene lamps hung on the walls in brackets with reflectors behind them. A large chandelier hung from the ceiling. This chandelier held twelve lamps similiar to the ones on the walls. It was the duty of the ladies to keep the lamps filled and shined.

Although the church was built in 1871, the deed was not written until the 8th of December, 1880. Dr. J.R. Morley sold the land to the trustees: J.R. Morley, James Conn, J.R. Earnest and Madison Campbell, for consideration of fifty dollars. The deed mentions the church now standing on this lot. The witnesses were Clay Shoun and Jas. F. Dotson.

The deed was written in 1880 but was not recorded until the 6th of May, 1886, in the Greene County Courthouse. W.H. Piper was the clerk of the court, and the deed is recorded in the registrar's office as follows.

This deed received at 12:00 o'clock of the 6th day of May 1886 duly certified and registered in said office No. 49, page 393, and noted in Book No. 3, Page 191.

Dr. Morley released all claim of this land to the Trustees to be held for the Methodist Episcopal Church South, covenant with said Trustees to forever PRESERVE AND DEFEND them in their right to said tract of land. From a list of donations made to the church in its early days we find Dr. Morley giving the sum of fifty dollars to the church returning the price paid him for the land.

The parsonage was the Shoun house, one of the oldest homes in the village. It is now over one hundred and thirty years old.

The church grew rapidly after its organization. Families from Rheatown, Chuckey, Afton, Limestone, and Pleasant Vale are recorded on the original record. By 1886 the membership had grown to 188.

As other Methodist Episcopal Churches South were organized in nearby communities, and members moved their membership to their local churches, the membership began to decline. By 1900 Limestone Church was the largest on the circuit, and the parsonage was moved there sometime before November 5th when the stewards of Rheatown Circuit met to set the salary for the minister, H.C. True. The salary was $400.00 for the year divided as follows: Limestone $150.00 Greenwood $105.00, Rheatown $85.00, Afton $60.00. James R. White, a charter member of the Rheatown Church, was recording secretary at this meeting.

Soon after this meeting the name of the circuit was changed to Limestone. Some of the churches were put on other circuits. Rheatown remained on Limestone Circuit until 1939. The churches on this circuit cooperated and often met for special services and revivals. The larger churches often contributed to the smaller ones to help them pay their conference obligations.

The ministers traveled on horse back or in buggies, taking the noon or evening meal with the members. When visiting in the community or holding protracted meetings (revivals), they stayed in the homes, often bringing their families with them.

The revivals were usually held in the winter when the farmers were not in their crops, with services both morning and evening. The attendance was good. People did not stay at home because it was cold. They wore warm clothes and sturdy shoes or boots, many of them made by the local cobblers. The women and children wore bearskin or homespun wool coats, suitable for the cold winter weather.

The men carried kerosene lanterns to guide their families to and from the services.

The people enjoyed the singing, prayers, testimonies, and long sermons and did not complain. It was a common occurance for a revival to continue for a month or longer, with many converted and rededicated.

A beautiful oak pump organ was played for the services. Among the organists remembered were Chloe Fisher, Emma Dukes, Opal Bright, Mary Donnelly, and Franke White. Among the song leaders after the turn of the century were James G. Keebler, Will Babb, Charles Hankal and Albert Baskette. Capt. J.J. Marshall was a frequent visitor amd was always invited to lead the singing.

The members appreciated the church and always contributed to its upkeep.

B. Clay Middleton once wrote the following to a Greeneville Newspaper: "Upon the right hand side of the road leading to Chuckey in Rheatown proper stands the Methodist Episcopal Church, South with a spire like a regular town church."

Sue Piper Thomas, born and reared in Rheatown, wrote the following about the church bell: "There is something about that old bell, its tones are so appealing, so beautiful and soothing. Bell making in the past was an art; some could get more from the old bell than others. Back in the early days of America bell ringing was handed down through generation from father to son.

"The bell in that day served for more than a signal to come to worship. It was used in times of some unusual event, in times of joy, gladness and times of distress when the help of neighbors were needed. The bell in the church near my home was one of the best toned I ever heard ring. On a clear Sabbath morning its tones echoed around the hills of the village and could be heard for miles."

The first hymnals (Methodist Hymnals) used in the church were very small and were printed without music like a poem or psalm. Mary Good White, wife of J.R.

Methodist Episcopal Church South, October 4, 1914

White, used one of these hymnals when a child.

The harp singers were a popular group during this period. They often met in the Rheatown Church, holding their meetings on Sunday afternoon. Led by Will Babb, they sang by note without a musical instrument.

The Methodists were always willing to share their building with other denominations. For many years, Sunday morning services were held in the Methodist Church, with services in the Presbyterian Church in the afternoon. Many families attended services in both churches. After the Presbyterian Church was condemned and closed, the Methodist Church shared their building with them until the church was built in Chuckey. Once each month their minister filled the pulpit. The Nick P. Earnest family attended these services.

Mrs. Earnest was a gifted musician and played for these services. Her father, Rev. Doggett, was a Presbyterian minister.

After the Presbyterian Church was completed in Chuckey, many of the Presbyterians in Rheatown continued to attend the Methodist Church. One lady, Miss Bessie McAdams, taught the card class for more than twenty years. Other Presbyterians attending included the McAdams family, Mrs. Julia Marshall, Mrs. Myrtle White and family, and the W.F. Piper family.

The quarterly meetings began on Saturday morning and continued through Sunday. Worship services were enjoyed morning and evening, with the charge business on the Saturday afternoon agenda. No business meetings were held on Sunday in those days.

The visitors from the churches on the charge were entertained in the homes of the members. The ladies were noted for their culinary achievements and were busy for days preparing delicious food for their guests. Ministers during the period of 1871 to 1939 were: E.R. Robertson, J.R. Chambers, K.D. Munsey, E.B. Moore, J.A. Bilderback, W.D. Mitchell, G.B. Draper, E.H. Boyle, J.D. Hickman, W.T. Fogleman, S.R. Morrell, J.W. Robertson, J.M. Walker, W.W. Pylatt, A.H. Lowe, J.C. Logan, W.C. Harris, A.T. Daily, John W. Hammer and Pat Horner.

Copy of Church register 1871-1909

All names are spelled as they are listed in the Church registers.

Barbara Argenbright	Sallie Argenbright	J.S. Anderson
Mike Anderson	Maude Argenbright	C.M. Argenbright
Gertrude Argenbright	A.W. Argenbright	W.H. Argenbright
Kitty Byerly	G.A. Bennett	Julia Bennett
W.C. Black	Barbara C. Black	Margaret Bicknell
Ida Byerly	Mary Byerly	Mary Black
Lillie C. Ripley (Birdwell)	Virginia Beales	William A. Bennett
F.F. Byerly	Bill Bennett	David Byerly
Charles Bennett	John Black	WIlliam Bair
Allen Black	Tenny Brumley	William Bowman
V.C. Bowman	Josie Berry	J.E. Birdwell
Lizzie Bowman	Florence Rupe Burgner	Mrs. M.E. Bogart
Barblay Black	W.H. Bail	Willie E. Birdwell
Henry R. Birdwell	Hubert A. Birdwell	Jas. E. Birdwell
J.W. Cox	Mariah Cox	J.R. Colling
John Conn	James Conn	Robert Conn
Madison Campbell	Fete Campbell	Lizzie Campbell
Alexander B. Campbell	D.F. Campbell	James Campbell
Charles Campbell	Mary Conn	Sally Carroll
John Campbell	David R. Craft	Fannie Cox
Elizabeth Campbell	Eddie Campbell	Bobbie Campbell
Henry Campbell	Elizabeth Chambers	C.R. Chambers
Mary E. Chambers	Scott Collette	Don Collette
Emma Campbell	Ada Campbell	Laura Campbell
A.H. Collett	Maggie Collett	Martha E. Collett
Lena Collett	Sallie Collett	Kate Campbell
H.H. Cox	Isaac Debusk	Mary Debusk
William Dukes	Roxanna Dukes	Robert Dukes
Racheal Davis	Lizzie Debusk	Rachel Debusk
Mary M. Dobson	Mary E. Dukes (Fisher)	Maggie E. Dukes (Rhey)
William M. Dukes, Jr.	Wmma Dukes (Bailey)	W.C. Durman
Martha E. Durman	W.F. Durman	J.O. Dukes
Nancy Moody Dukes	J.R. Earnest	Isaac Earnest
Victoria B. Earnest	J.E. Earnest	H.C. Earnest
W.A. Earnest	J.H. Earnest	Mattie L. Earnest

Betty B. Earnest	Florence Earnest	Lamyer C. Ellott
W.R. Earnest	D.V. Earnest	H.D. Fraker
Sarah Fraker	P.W. Ford	H.E. Ford
Fredrick Fraker	Dinah Fraker	A.B. Fullen
Eliza Fullen	J.C. Fisher	Lanak T. Fisher
Earnest Fraker	Emma Fraker	Amanda Fraker
H.H. Ford	Annia C. Fullen	John Fullen
Gertrude Fraker Marshall	J.O. Fullen	J.H. Fisher
George Fullen	Ann Fullen	W.C. Francis
John Hice	Elizabeth Hice	Alice Hice Cox
Vic Hice	Lulu Hice	Mariah K. Hikay
Willis Hubbard	Steler Scott Hill	Maude Howell
William Hubbard	Charles Huffaker	Gordan Huffaker
Jo Ella Huffaker	Ada Huffaker	Robt. O. Huffaker
Edd Huffaker	Wm. Johnson	Cordia Johnson
Mrs. Wm. Johnson	Nina Johnson	Winel Johnson
William Liebes	Viola Kelsay	Judith Liebes
1886 James Kelsey	G.F. Libes	James C. Keebler
Lewis C. Libes	Mary S. Keebler	Charles J. Lane
Mollie Liebs	A.H. Liebs	Junath Liebs
J.C. Liebs	L.C. Leeth	Adelia Smith
Mary Scott	J.F. Stphens	Emma Stphens
Lizzie T. Shoun	Lidia Spangler	Henry Smith
Dicie L. Smith	1886 Stellar Scott	W.L. Smith
Joseph J. Skinnell	Mary A. Skinnell	Frances Smith
Eulalia Shoun	Jessie Scott	Edjar Sellars
Jennie Thompson	J.R. Morley	Rachel Morley
William D. Morrison	Martha L. Martin	Minnie L. Moore
Mary E. Moore	James W. Moore	Thomas Morgan
Mary R. Mitchell	N. Pearl Mitchell	M.A. McIntosh
Maggie McIntosh	J.G. Nelson	J.H. Nightshirk
G.W. Nelson	Adaline Nelson	J.M. Naff
Mrs. L.F. Naff	Laura Bell Oakes	Nancy Pickering
H.E. Patton	M. Belle Patton	J.R. Pope
Mollie Pope	Eddie Patton	Pearl Penix
Georgia L. Rhea	Margaret Ripley	Mary J. Robertson
Cora F. Robinson	Frank Ripley	Frank Robertson
William H. Ripley	A.W. Rupe	J.S. Rhea
Mrs. E.B. Robertson	Miss Annie Robertson	William H. Ripley
Mrs. A.W. Rupe	Will Rupe	Mrs. Will Rupe
Walter Rothrock	Mollie Rothrock	Ada Ripley
Jns. W. Ragsdell L.P.	W.G. Rothrock	W.M. Richardson
Belle Richardson	Addie Richardson	Edward Ripley
Mary Reeser	Bill Richardson	Elizabeth White
J.R. White	Mattie V. White	T.N. Weems

Mary E. Weems	James Williams	H.K. White
James Hice Williams	Liza C. Wilson	Lulu White
Will White	Henry White	Carl White
J.C. Zimmerman	S.J. Zimmerman	Minnie H. White

Members Added: 1909-1939

Cleo Argenbright	Isabelle Barnes	Opal Barnes
Elmer Barnes	Mary Babb	Mabel Babb
Roxie Babb	Jessie Barnes	Bronce Barnes
Franke White	Carrie Bradley	Lawrence Bradley
Ralph Bradley	Rowena Bradley	Lucille Bradley
C.G. Burger	Mrs. C.G. Burger	Lura Burger
Doris Burger	Bertha Naff Baskette	Annie Collette
Charley Collette	Mary Campbell	Bessie Denney
Nina Denney	Flora Denney	Elbert Denney
Rosa Dyer	Mollie Dyer	Fannie Dotson
Irene Fisher	Ollie Fisher	Campbell Fisher
May Fisher	Ralph Fisher	Marie Finkle
Gladys Finkle	M.Z. Furches	Ella May Furches
Haskell Furches	Ben F. Gregory	Orgille Gregory
Allen Henry	Effie Hankal	James Keebler
Joseph Keebler	Irene Keebler	Clara Keebler
W.S. Lilly	Odie Lilly	Paul Marshall
Frank McAmis	Glen McAmis	Addie McAmis
Mrs. Frank McAmis	J. Randall Moody	Cecil Moody
Earnest F. Moody	Glenna Rodgers	Delia Rodgers
Andy Pitts	Jimmy Pitts	Henderson Rodgers
Laura Rodgers	J. Newt Range	Clara Range
Samuel Range	James Earl Thomas	Mary Emily Thomas
Mary E. White		

Guy Thomas (Preparatory member)

Rheatown Methodist Church

The Methodist Church merged in 1939 and the Rheatown church went on the Clear Springs Charge with Clear Springs, Liberty Hill, Milburnton, and Pleasant Grove.

Our parsonage was near the Clear Springs Church. It was an old house, and a few years later a modern brick parsonage was built. Many years of Christian fellowship were enjoyed with the people of the five churches when we met quarterly in charge-wide board meetings to plan our work and fellowship together. The churches on the circuit often came together for programs, revivals, and fellowship meetings.

We were fortunate to have Geraldine Hunt, a Methodist rural worker, to work with the churches for four years. She gave us encouragement and help in every department. The children and youth were drawn to her by her nice personality and Christian witness. Membership in Methodist Youth Fellowship increased; church school and worship services were well attended. Miss Hunt was a gifted pianist and singer and was always willing to use her talents. Although it has been years since Geraldine was here, we will always remember the unselfish and lasting contribution she made to our church.

Although the church retains the original structure, over a period of years many changes have been made in the interior. The first improvement was the removal of the large coal heater which was replaced with two modern gas furnaces. In 1957 ceiling, walls, and floors were replaced, and the church was insulated; part of the front of the large sanctuary was enclosed, making four classrooms. All the work was donated by the Men's Bible Class.

When the new church furniture was purchased, the two aisles were changed to a center aisle, and the two entrance doors were replaced by one double door.

An active Young Adult Group was organized. Their projects were to raise the money to purchase a much-needed aisle carpet and an altar rail. Their efforts were a success. In a short time, the beautiful red carpet and altar rail were purchased.

Pastors from 1939 to 1968 included: J.M. Dew, Guy Fleenor, John Smith, Kenner W. Baldwin, Leonard Churchwell, Thurman Littreal, Howard Griffith, Charles Lindholm, P.A. Hawkins, and James Adcox.

Members Added to Church Roll: 1939-1969

Linda Adams	Janie Adams	William A. Bolinger
Mary Bolinger	Flora Bolinger	William (Billy) Bolinger
Cordie Bolinger	Helen Bolinger	Shannon Bolinger
James H. (Jim) Balding	Nelle Britton	Mary Chase
Romaine Collette	Eugene Cooter	Dewey Furches
Mabre Furches	Mrs. Olive Hudson	Thomas Hudson
Edna Hilton	Ronnie Hilton	Donnie Hilton
Velt Hilton	Robert Harmon	Radford Jones
Alex Jordan	Amanda Jordan	James Laws
W.F. Lewis	Barbara Laws	Frances Laws
Jimmie Ruth Laws	Jeannie Laws	Charles Monk
Helen McCurry	Bonnie McLean	Peggy McCurry
Mae McIntosh	Brownlow McIntosh	Aldon McIntosh
Robert McIntosh	Joan McIntosh	Lawrence McIntosh
Caroline Malone	Oliver L. "Jack" McCurry	Wanda Monk
Roy Monk	Marjorie Phillips	Mary Ethel Ricker
Mary Martha Phillips	Betty Phillips	Evaleen Rodgers
James D. Rodgers	Mary Sue Rodgers	Robert Rodgers
Frances Ragsdale	Judy Ragsdale	Jerry Ragsdale
Jane Ragsdale	Mary Jo Solomon	Harlin Sexton
Dorothy Sexton	Mrs. Edith Thomas	Newell Thomas

Preparatory members:
James H. Balding, Jr.   Beverly Monk

Members Added Since 1969

Emma Campbell	Margaret Daugherty	Hope Dyer
Elmer Daugherty	Pauline Daugherty	Ina Hinkle
Irene Daugherty	Clarence Doyle	David Monk
Joseph Daugherty	Dorothy Doyle	Jerry Thomas
Lorene Daugherty	Earl Doyle	Preparatory Member:
Lowell Daugherty	Lou Doyle	Lee Anna Sullivan

THE SHOUN HOUSE *The Shoun House has been the home to many families since its construction. Some of the families that have lived here are Shouns, Earle Thomas, Bolingers (Henry Bolinger came back from a short stay in Minnesota in 1912 and remodeled this house.), Mrs. Julia Marshall, Ed Wills, Rev. W.H. Turner, and Newt Range. Kennith Huffman is the present owner.*

Rheatown United Methodist Church

After the merger of the United Brethren Evangelical and Methodist Churches on April 23, 1968, the Rheatown Church went on the Otterbein Circuit. The circuit has four churches — Albright, Rheatown, Union Temple, and Jearoldstown.

Since 1969 the old roof has been replaced with a new one and a new siding added to the rear of the church. The only change in the interior of the church has been the hanging of red velvet draperies in the sanctuary. The building is in good condition. The present trustees are James H. Balding, Charles Monk, and John Hite.

The parsonage is located in Rheatown near the Albright Church. Harlan Sexton is the parsonage trustee.

The highlights of 1976 were the ringing of the historical old church bell for the 200th birthday of the nation on Sunday, July 4, 1976, when bells all over the nation rang for a period of 10 minutes at 2:00 p.m., and the celebration of the 105th anniversary of the church on November 28th, 1976, with a bicentennial program and open house, featuring an historical display of church records and pictures of the church since its organization. Included in the display were many relics, some over one hundred years old.

Among those present were three of six generations of church membership: Helen Thomas McCurry, Peggy McCurry Balding, and Amy and Jimmy Balding. The other three generations were Elizabeth Morley White, the great-great grandmother of Mrs. Balding; James Randolph White, son of Mrs. White; and Lulu White Thomas, daughter of James White and mother of Mrs. McCurry. Dave and Becky Monk represented the fourth generation of the Daugherty membership. Pauline Daugherty Monk, mother of David and Becky, was also present. The other two generations were Mrs. Margaret Jordan Daugherty and Rev. Joseph A. Daugherty, father and grandmother of Mrs. Monk. The third generation of the Rodgers family, Robert and Mary Sue Rodgers, were present. The other two generations were Henderson F. Rodgers, father of James D. (Jimmy) Rodgers, father of Robert and Mary Sue.

The comfortable and beautiful sanctuary we enjoy worshipping in today has been made possible by the liberal contributions of members and memorial gifts of relatives and friends. Some of these generous people live in far away places but are still interested in the small country church they attended in their youth.

Harry E. Thomas has been pastor of the Rheatown Methodist Church since 1969.

MEMBERS UNITING: 1969-1977

James Russell Alexander	Laura Elizabeth Prescott
Kathy Isom Alexander	Rex Stanton
Amy Kathryn Balding	Deborah Stoner
James J. (Jimmy) Balding, Jr.	Joseph Stoner
Andrea Thomas Prescott Campbell	Patricia Stoner
Ada Cooley	Peggy Jean Stoner
Bo Cooley	Ralph Stoner
Roberta Lynn Pitts Cooter	Kathleen Watts
Jeannie Hite	Michael Watts
Rebecca Hite	Ollie Wolfe
Tyler James Laws	
Lena Mae Malone	Preparatory member:
Betty Moore McIntoch	
Cindy Michelle McIntosh	Amy Kathryn Balding
Michael Robert McIntosh	Joey Fayette Cooter
Rebecca Monk	Lorinda Lynn Cooter

Elizabeth Ann (Morley) White (1824-1884), who started the first Methodist Sunday School in Rheatown.

Sunday School

The church school with training in Methodism has always been emphasized in our church. The first Sunday School was organized under the leadership of Elizabeth Morley White, before the church was built in 1871. The earliest record we have of the Sunday School is dated 1911. Joe D. Keebler (Uncle Joe) was superintendent, with Henry Bolinger assistant, the organist was Franke White, and assistant, Opal Bright. Song leaders were Will Babb and J.H. Myers.

The number enrolled at this time was seventy, with a good average attendance. The offerings were from four cents to forty-five cents. The cost of the literature averaged $2.50 per quarter.

The secretary recorded the hymns, prayers, scripture read, and the weather for the day.

Other superintendents from 1912 to the present included: Major R.H.M. Donnelly, J.M. Naff, Henderson F. Rodgers, J. Newt Range, Frank McAmis, J. Elbert Denney, Jimmy Rodgers, and James Balding. Robert McIntosh is our present superintendent. Assistants are Robert Rodgers and Charles Monk.

We are still enjoying Sunday School in our church today. Perhaps we are reaping the harvest other Christians have sown before us. Each of us has known people in our church who by their lives, words, and songs still live among us, although they have passed from this life. Their message is still with us and we, as members of the Rheatown United Methodist Sunday School, are reapers of their faith today.

The Methodist Women's Organizations

LADIES AID: in 1920 the ladies of the Rheatown Episcopal Methodist Church South organized the Ladies Aid. This was an active group. The charter members were: Minnie Keebler, Lulu Thomas, Franke White, Clara Keebler, Clara Range, Cleo Argenbright, Effie Hankal, Mary Donnelly, Bessie McAdams, and Carrie Bradley.

One of their first projects was to raise money to purchase a piano for the sanctuary. To finance this project, the ladies gave a religious play. The play was well received in the local church, and they were invited to give it in other communities. With their offerings, they purchased the piano we use today, for $100.00. During this period, homemade ice cream, cake, pie, and box suppers were a popular way to raise money for the church.

WOMEN'S SOCIETY OF CHRISTIAN SERVICE: Later a part of the charter members, with some younger women, organized Women's Society of Christian Service. New members of this organization were: Cordie Bolinger, Flora Bolinger, Amanda Jordan, Margaret Daugherty, Irene Daugherty, Mary Chase, Olive Curtain, Edna Hilton, Ina Smith, Helen McCurry, Evaleen Rodgers, Mae McIntosh, Eppie Stanton, Dorothy Sexton, Barbara Laws, Pauline Monk, and Peggy Balding.

No record was kept of the number of quilts sold by this energetic group, who were always joined by Bess Milburn and Velva Wills when they had a quilting bee. Friendship quilts were made and sold to add to the treasury. Most of their projects were supported by the members' pledges, with gifts contributed by friends and former members. Money from these projects was used to support both the local church and missions.

UNITED METHODIST WOMEN: We are now United Methodist Women with ten active members meeting monthly. We use the recommended literature, emphasizing missions and support of local church projects. New members of this group are: Nancy Sexton, Kathleen Watts, Mary Sue Rodgers, Rebecca Monk, Mary Wolfe, Nova Tranbarger, and Mary Martha Hite.

In 1976 two of our members attended U.M.W. Annual Conference in Bristol, Virginia. Five members attended the District meeting in Elizabethton, Tennessee, to plan our work for 1977. We are honored to have one of our members, Pauline Monk, elected Secretary of Program Resources for the District this year — 1977.

Our long range project is restoring the spire to our old church. To finance this project we are publishing this book. The sum from the sale of the books will be added to our steeple fund.

Albright United Methodist Church
by
Mildred Bowman Jeffers

In 1926 the Tennessee United Brethren Conference bought the brick building, built in 1856, from the Presbyterians. Rev. J.A. Johnson organized the congregation with thirty-four members. The first trustees were Albert Baskette, Frank Fisher, and Charlie Brown. Rev. W.H. Turner was assigned as pastor in 1927 and served two years. Rev. C.W. Rightsell became pastor in 1930 and served five years. Other pastors have been Rev. George Richardson, Rev. R.H. Birthright, Rev. Lee A. Cate, Rev. Glen Cox, Rev. Don White, Rev. Kenneth Huff, Rev. Charles Mason, Rev. Leo Bulson, and Rev. Harry Thomas (the present pastor).

Conference Evangelist, Dr. Dewey Whitwell, conducted several successful revivals, and as a result, many members were received into the church.

Two pastors in the Tennessee Conference are products of this church, Rev. E.B. Jeffers and Rev. Dwight Kenney. Two Sunday School classmates of Rev. Kenney are pastors in other denominations. They are Rev. Robert Dixon and Rev. James Bowers. Rev. Jeffers is the son of Dr. E.A. and Mrs. Phronia Jeffers. Rev. Kenney is the son of George and Fleta Kenney and grandson of Dr. and Mrs. Jeffers. Rev. Dixon is the son of Bill and Anna Mae Dixon, and Rev. Bowers is the son of Denver and Adelee Bowers.

In 1952 an educational unit was added to the back of the church.

On November 16, 1946, the United Brethren and Evangelical Churches were merged at General Conference in Johnstown, Pennsylvania. We became the Evangelical United Brethren Church.

On April 23, 1968, the E.U.B. Churches and the Methodist churches were merged at General Conference, and now are the Albright United Methodist Church of the Holston Methodist Conference, with Rev. L. Scott Allen as Bishop and Rev. Raymond White as Conference Superintendent.

In the spring of 1972, the old brick structure was demolished, and a new brick building was built in with the educational unit. The first service was held in the new sanctuary on December 3, 1972.

The dedication service was held August 24, 1975, with Bishop L. Scott Allen, Supt. James Green, and Rev. Harry Thomas performing the ceremony.

THE REV. JAMES FISHER HOUSE *The Rev. James Fisher family occupied this house for many years. Others living there were the Hankins, Bowlin, and the Rome Collette families.*

MAJOR WILLIAM C. SCOTT

Written by A.C. Ketron and contributed by Mrs. Victor Southwood of Indianapolis, Indiana. Mrs. Southwood is the granddaughter of Major Scott. This was the write-up about her grandfather when he died. Her grandmother died soon after his death. Those who knew her best said she grieved to death.

William C. Scott was born August 17, 1847, in Rheatown, Tennessee, and from this little town in which he spent most of his earthly life, he departed to the Spirit World on March 17, 1915.

On October 12, 1863, he enlisted as a soldier in Company K, Eighth Tennessee Cavalry Federal Army and was honorably discharged September 11, 1865. He was then returned to his father's home and remained there until his father's death which occurred in 1869. After this he and his brother took charge of the family of seven children.

He was married to Lydia Ellis November 11, 1875. The other children, with their good mother, still survive. Brother Scott was an honest man, hardworking, and an upright Christian gentleman, loved and respected by his neighbors and friends. He was kind and accommodating to rich and poor alike. In the home he was always a good husband and father. About forty-five years ago under the ministry of Rev. John R. Hughes, he was converted and joined the church, and from thence he tried to live the life of the Christian until the day of his death.

Brief funeral services were conducted in the home by the writer of this sketch, assisted by Rev. F.M. Cones of Chuckey and Rev. Logan of Limestone, after which the body was laid to rest in the old country cemetery at Rheatown, Tennessee — there to await the resurrection of the just.

Truly we are made to believe that he tried to obey the junction of Him who said, "Be thou faithful unto death and I will give thee a crown of life."

Trees are an important part of the landscape in any community. In building roads — especially the early roads — man spared a stately tree if it was at all possible. The two towering sugar maples just south of Rheatown on the Chuckey Road are a good example of this. Hanging on the bank along the road, they have withstood the elements and are still a beautiful sight, especially in the autumn.

Trees are the highest form of plant life on this earth, and some live to be of great size and age. This stately oak stands just off the Chuckey road on the Dave Grant farm. It stands there in its rugged beauty as a sentinel to the passing years. Many a farm animal has found its boughs a place of refreshing shade. Kilmer was correct in saying, "Only God can make a tree."

Captain J.J. Marshall (1865-1943)

CAPTAIN J.J. MARSHALL

One of Rheatown's most colorful characters was Joseph John Marshall, or Captain J.J. Marshall, as he was most affectionately known. Captain Marshall was born September 10, 1865, the son of Eli and Rebecca Jones Marshall of Rheatown. His friends being of the Quaker faith sent their son to the New Hope school in Quaker Knobs and later to the Rheatown Academy. Capt. Marshall began his college training at the Earlhome Quaker College in Indiana, returning a year later to complete his education at Tusculum. According to the 1889 commencement program, there were seven graduates in his class.

After graduation Capt. Marshall entered the mercantile business by purchasing a small drugstore in Rheatown. However, the store burned in 1893 or 1894. His next business took him to the Fairview community where he operated another store. Again this business lasted only a short while and in 1899 he bought a farm near Clear Springs. For the next forty-four years Captain Marshall spent his time working on his farm.

Agriculture was not the Captain's sole interest. He was very active in the military. During the late 1800's he joined the National Guard and participated for a period of time each year in practice exercises. From 1916-1917 he was assigned to the Mexican border. He was discharged from the third Tennessee infantry in 1888.

This service earned him the rank of captain. From this time on he was known as Capt. J.J. by his many friends. Capt. J.J. desperately wanted to serve in active duty in World War I, but his acceptance papers arrived just a few days after Armistice.

Capt. Marshall was also very much involved in community and church life. For forty years he served as Superintendent of the Clear Springs Sunday School, which he had also helped to organize. Captain loved to sing and was an active member of the Harp Singers. He belonged to the Odd Fellows Lodge for years. He was very interested in history, especially local history, and wrote an article on Rheatown for **News Bulletin** and **Greeneville Sun** for a number of years. Being of a jovial disposition, he joked and played tricks on his many friends and was always a welcome addition to any community gathering.

Captain J.J. was also a family man. On December 21, 1892, he married Gertrude Fraker, daughter of Dr. W.E. and Emma Morley Fraker. Rev. John Hixon, the Methodist minister of Rheatown, performed the ceremony. To this union was born one son, Paul, who is now deceased, and two daughters, Thelma and Dorothy. Thelma married Fred Campbell, and resides near the original Marshall home. They have two sons, Earl and Robert (Bob), and several grandchildren. The youngest daughter, Dorothy, is a retired school teacher and lives in Limestone. She and her mother moved to Limestone after the death of Mr. Marshall.

Captain Marshall died December 9, 1943, at his Clear Springs home and was laid to rest in the Mt. Bethel Cemetery.

Gertrude (Fraker) Marshall (1872-1968), wife of Captain J.J. Marshall and daughter of Dr. and Mrs. W.E. Fraker.

JAMES DANA RODGERS
by
Mary Sue Rodgers

James Dana Rodgers, known to most people as Jimmy, was born on December 6, 1908, to Rev. Henderson F. and Laura Rodgers. They lived in a small frame house in the upper end of Rheatown, along with his four half sisters, Delia, Mellie, Glenna, and Mae. He had one other half sister, Mary, who died when she was a year old.

He attended his first year of school at Rheatown Academy. After the school burned he attended Oakdale.

His father had to be away from home a lot due to his ministry, which meant that Jimmy had to begin farming at a very young age. He continued to farm all of his life. He took a lot of pride in his Hereford cattle and his crops. He was a firm believer in putting nutrients back into the soil. He took a strong interest in raising sweet potatoes and sweet potato plants. He sold plants to people far and near. The largest crop of sweet potatoes that he raised was one hundred and seventy-five bushels from one-half acre of ground. He bedded as many as sixty bushels each spring.

He raised tobacco, corn, and other crops common to East Tennessee area farmers.

He was married on August 12, 1951, to Evaleen Lady. They had two children, Mary Sue and Robert.

Rev. Henderson F. Rodgers (1871-1947), wife Laura (1880-1950), seated, and James Dana Rodgers (1908-1971). The woman standing and the baby are not identified.

He attended the Rheatown United Methodidt Church beginning in his childhood, and continued to serve as a faithful member all of his life. He held various offices in the church and served as superintendent for twenty years and was superintendent at the time of his death. He was elected magistrate of Rheatown and served for nearly eleven years.

He died on May 15, 1971 of a heart attack. The memory of his quiet but easygoing nature will long linger in the pages of the minds of those who knew him.

THE REV. H.F. RODGERS HOUSE *The Rev. H.F. Rodgers built this house after the turn of the century and raised a large family there. The property is still owned by the heirs of his son, Jimmy.*

WILLIAM F. PIPER

William F. Piper was born at Tusculum on September 4, 1867. He was the youngest of the three sons of Charles Wesley and Sue W. Remine Piper. Charles Wesley Piper, his father, served as First Lieutenant in Company C., 4th Tennessee Infantry, during the Civil War. His father later became Postmaster at Tusculum. William Piper's grandfather and grandmother were Albert Morgan Piper and Martha O. Allen Piper.

Albert Piper had been a merchant in Rogersville as early as 1838, but later moved to Knoxville to become a clerk and partner in the Coffin Bros. firm. He later became a partner of S.B. Boyd, a Knoxville merchant. In 1858 he became Mayor of Knoxville. A few years later, Albert Piper bought a farm and became a Greene County merchant. In 1871, he became a United States Deputy Revenue Collector. Albert Piper died June 11, 1878, the first victim of cholera of that year. Both he and his wife are buried in the Rheatown Cemetery. It is quite possible that Martha O. Allen's family was among the first Rheatown settlers, since the names are the same.

William F. Piper entered the printing trade at the age of thirteen. This trade helped him work his way through Tusculum College, where he graduated in 1888 at the age of sixteen.

After college, William F. Piper became a teacher in Greene County, Tennessee. He taught at Liberty Hill, Clear Springs, Chuckey, and Rheatown. When Joel Pierce was superintendent, he begged Piper to "come across the river and help teach some boys who have run every teacher we've had away." Piper went across the river (name of settlement not known) and had no trouble. He was even able to board there for fifty cents per week.

William Piper, in those years, was the highest paid teacher in Greene County, receiving as much as thirty dollars per month. He was best known as a beloved teacher at Rheatown Academy, where he taught a number of years. There he was to meet and marry one of his students, Mary Susanna Keebler, the daughter of Joseph D. and Sarah Jane Bright Keebler. They were married in Rheatown on June 6, 1889.

For a short period of time, the Pipers left Rheatown and went to Newport where he taught school. During his teaching years, W.F. Piper continued to run a print shop to supplement their income. Piper left teaching to become a newpaper publisher.

W.F. Piper founded the Rheatown, Tennessee **Rural Searchlight**, but later was to move this paper to Greeneville to combine with the **Greeneville Sun**. From Greeneville he went to Limestone to publish the **Limestone Enterprise**, then later to Jonesborough to publish the **Jonesborough Herald and Tribune**.

Mr. Piper then became city editor on the **Comet**, the first daily published in Johnson City. Later, he was to publish the Bluff City **Sullivan County Developer**.

In 1919 W.F. Piper moved his family to Elizabethton, Tennessee. There he leased the **Carter County Banner** from the Fitzsimmons family until 1926. In 1926 he founded and published the **Elizabethton News**, a weekly, which he was to publish until 1936. From 1936 to 1939 he published and edited the **Elizabethton Times**.

W.F. Piper moved to Johnson City, Tennessee, in 1942 when his daughter, Sue Piper Thomas, joined the news staff of the **Press-Chronicle**. There he was to operate a printing shop until his death in 1952 at the age of eighty-five years.

Mr. and Mrs. Piper had four children: Sue Remine, Joseph, Rachel, and Mary Magdaline. Joseph and Rachel died when children.

Mr. Piper was a Presbyterian, a life-long Republican, and a member of the Odd Fellows. He was also a charter member of the Tennessee Press Association and served as president of that group in 1929.

THE WILL PIPER HOUSE *The Piper house stands near the store and Rheatown United Methodist Church. Other families who have occupied this house includes Buford and Sue Thomas, Jess and Nelle Brink, and Phillip and Wilma Peters. It is now occupied by Terry Wampler, son of George Wampler.*

JAMES R. "JIMMY" WHITE

James R. "Jimmy" White, son of Isaac and Elizabeth Morley White, born near St. Clair in Hawkins County, March 12, 1853, was a fixture in Rheatown for many years. His father died when Jimmy was a young lad. His mother, wishing to be near her brother, Dr. J.R. Morley, and other relatives, bought a small farm in the lower end of Rheatown and moved here with her four children, James R., Keene, Charley and Mattie.

Jimmy married Mary "Mollie" Good, daughter of Hartsell and Martha Milburn Good. Mollie had two brothers, Hartsell and Will Good. Jimmy and Mollie settled in Rheatown on Main Street, where they raised their family. There were nine children — four daughters, Minnie, Lulu, Elizabeth (Lizzie), and Franke, and three sons, Will, Henry, and Carl; a daughter and son died in infancy.

For many years Jimmy sold Singer sewing machines and monuments, traveling over the county in his buggy or riding a horse. He would spend the night wherever he happened to be at the end of the day. Many of the sewing machines he sold are still in use in the Rheatown community and surrounding areas.

Jimmy, an ardent Democrat, was elected magistrate of Rheatown when he was a young man and served in the Greene County Court for over fifty years. Thus, he acquired the name "Squire White". He maintained an office in his home and conducted his business there. Trials were usually held in one of the stores. If a couple wanted him to marry them, he asked some of his family to witness the ceremony.

"Squire Jimmy" always walked to Chuckey to catch the early morning train to Greeneville. The last few years he served as magistrate, he would don his white shirt and stiff collar the night before, in order to dress more quickly the next morning. His daughters and grandchildren had many laughs about this incident.

A quiet man of few words, "Squire Jimmy" loved his family and was usually surrounded by some of his twenty-three grandchildren. Always interested in com-

J.R. White House

munity affairs, Jimmy was a Master Mason and a member of the Odd Fellows Lodge.

"Squire Jimmy" had two hobbies — reading and walking. He was an avid reader of the Bible, his church papers, and the daily newspapers. It was not unusual for him to walk to Chuckey in the afternoon to get the mail. When the weather was too rough for him to walk to Chuckey, one of his grandchildren would pick up his mail after school and deliver it to him.

He was a charter member of the Rheatown Methodist Church South and was active in church work until a few months before his death, September 4, 1935, at the age of eighty-two years. James R. Bailes, son of Mr. and Mrs. Carl Bailes of Knoxville, Tennessee, and great grandson of "Squire Jimmy", is a United Methodist Minister now serving in Holston Conference.

James Randolph White (1852-1935), Mary Emily (Good) White (1859-1926), and daughter Lulu Morley White (1887-1971).

ONE WAY OF REMEMBERING RHEATOWN
by
William H. Slagle

As a lad, I often took walks from my home in Rheatown. One day during 1917, as I was passing the house two doors from my house, I noticed an old man rocking on his front porch. He was not the type to yell across the road and speak, but a very warm, quiet gentleman as I remember him. I had often wondered why people referred to him as "Squire White," so I decided to ask him about it. I sat down on the steps and asked him if "Squire White" was a nickname or if it was really his name.

"Squire White" got out of his rocker, came over, sat on the steps, and explained the title. He said that "Squire" was an elected county or village official, and that "Squires" had several duties to render to the community or village from which they were elected.

I suppose that when I asked him about "Squire" that he was probably sitting there day dreaming of the old town, Rheatown, as it had been seventy to one hundred years prior.

After about an hour of stories, he stood up and invited me into his home. In a desk in the corner of his living room, he pulled out an old key and told me the following story:

> For years up to about 1895 or 1896, the Calaboose was located in a room under the store on the corner of the Chuckey and the Stage Coach Road. The Calaboose was a room with all four walls made of stone, and two doors, one of steel and one of wood. The Calaboose was used to lock up troublemakers for a night, and then they were transferred to Greeneville the following day.

The old gentleman handed me the key and told me to keep it so I would be sure to remember the story of a village, Rheatown, that had seen its glory.

Franke White and Helen M. Thomas playing in a stream with the Rheatown Calaboose in the background.

THE RHEATOWN POST OFFICE *was the scene of much activity in the days of the horse-mounted mail carrier. Mail was brought here by stage coach and later from the local train at Chuckey.*

After the discontinuance of its use as a Post Office it was used as a garage for the first car which was owned by Jim Keebler. It was an "Allen" car.

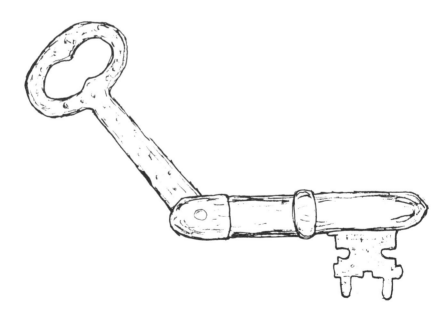

Rheatown Calaboose Key

HAPPY MEMORIES
by
Mary Thomas Sullivan

Today I visited the historic Rheatown Cemetery. It is fifty years since my father, William Earle Thomas, was laid to rest. I was only seven, and shared his birthday, July 16. Memory of him is faint, except I well remember that his birthday gifts to me were always very special, and he made an effort to be at home from his trips as a salesman for the Sunbeam Furnace Company.

As the years passed by, it was a very special, close relationship that I enjoyed with my mother, Lulu White Thomas; my father's mother, Martha Baxter Reams, who lived with us; my sister, Helen; brother-in-law, Jack McCurry; and brothers, Reamer, Earl, Guy, and Jack. Also I was blessed by having a dear grandfather, J.R. White, with whom I was always near and sought guidance from his wealth of wisdom and practical experience. My Aunt Franke White was just like a second mother, sewing for me and teaching me all the little details of running a household. I lived with them most of the time after my father died, until I was graduated from high school in 1935.

During my high school years, I treasure also being near to Aunt Minnie White Keebler, her daughter Irene Rowe and her husband Walter. My very dear friends included members of the Jeffers family, especially Willard, Clarice, and Rex; the Bolinger family; the Turner family; the Ranges; and other members of our two local churches, the Rheatown Methodist Church (which I joined at the age of 10) and the United Brethren Church as well. In those days my friends and I had no problem being busy and happy with our church work. Our people of today cannot possibly understand the simple, but gratifying, life we led in our little village.

Since I married Bill Sullivan, a native Kentuckian, in 1944, I have lived in ten states and raised six children, and Bill has just retired after 27 years with the F.B.I. We give most of the credit for our success to the encouragement we always received from my mother. She was loving, kind, unselfish, and anxious only for us to be happy. Our children all love and remember the fun they had visiting in her lovely country farm house. We now live in Los Angeles, California. Our children are scattered, except Martha, 17, who is at home and a senior in high school — Mrs. Michael Elliott (Lee Anna), Sacramento, California; Chris Thomas and his wife, Patricia, in Chicago, Illinois; Lt. (j.g.) William Ted, U.S. Navy, Pearl Harbor; John Robert, University of Kentucky; and Donald Joseph, University of Missouri.

It is always heart-warming to return to Rheatown, visit and relive all the happy memories of the past. The next visit, I hope to see the new spire atop the Methodist Church — my first church — dear to my heart and a symbol of happy association with Christian friends and relatives.

ULIS M. BRADLEY HOUSE *Built by Mr. Bradley in 1909, Mr. and Mrs. Bradley resided here for fifty-five years until he retired from farming and moved to Tusculum.*

LAWRENCE BRADLEY HOUSE *This house was built by Mr. Bradley, and the family resided here for many years before moving to the Haws Cross Road community. This house is now owned by Mrs. Joe Swanay.*

ROBERT F. RODGERS
RECEIVES HIGHEST FFA DEGREE

At the time of publication, Mr. Robert F. Rodgers, son of Evaleen Lady Rodgers and the late James D. Rodgers had been nominated to receive the American Farmer degree, which is the highest award to be received by a member of the Future Farmers of America.

Rodgers earned the American Farmers degree on the basis of his farm work in beef cattle, tobacco, corn, hay, and pasture production, etc.

Currently Rodgers is serving as Assistant Superintendent of the Rheatown United Methodist Church and a member of the board of directors of the Limestone Ruritan Club.

RANGE STORE *The frame store building generally known as the "Range Store" was the scene of much activity when Rheatown was a busy trading center. Newt Range had a store here prior to 1916, then H.V. Bolinger sold goods there until his death in 1921. During the cold winter of 1917, there was a flu epidemic and many capsules of quinine would be taken home and all the family would join in making capsules to be sold the next day. Other owners were E.E. Ripley and Albert Baskette. Jerry Thomas purchased this building and moved it across the road, where he was a merchant for several years. Jerry also had a rolling store which he sold to Jack Thomas and Jimmy Massengill. Oscar Wolfe purchased the store and operated it until his retirement. It was then purchased by his brother, Ralph, who owned it when it burned in 1975.*

John Newton Range (1874-1950) and Clara Winslow Range (1880-1971) on their wedding day.

Dr. W.E. Fraker (1851-1908)

Tullie M. Shoun (1883-1947)

Duncan Reesen Thomas (1848-1897) and wife Mattie (Baxter) Thomas (1857-1944). Mattie married M.J. Reams after the death of Duncan.

Parlor in Mattie (Baxter) Thomas Reams House, built in 1876

Henry V. Bolinger (1871-1921) and Cordelia L. Bolinger (1874-1947) on their wedding day.

Children of Henry Valentine Bolinger and Cordelia Fellers Bolinger around 1907-1908, left to right: Mary Ruth, Lillie May and William Alexander.

NAME INDEX

NAME INDEX

NAME INDEX

NAME INDEX

Rhea, Maggie, 64
Rhea, Samuel, 71
Rhea, Vess, 16
Richardson, Addie, 77
Richardson, Belle, 77
Richardson, Bill, 77
Richardson, Billie, 25
Richardson, George (Rev.), 85
Richardson, John H., 64
Richardson, Lily Dale, 64
Richardson, Rebecca Isabelle, 64
Richardson, W.M., 77
Richardson, William Melton, 64
Ricker, Mary Ethel, 80
Ricker, Raleigh, 13
Ricker, Selma, 13
Ricker, Selma Hankal, 11
Riddle, John, 72
Rightsell, C.W. (Rev.), 85
Rimel, 24
Ripley, Ada, 77
Ripley, Argel, 3
Ripley, David, 71
Ripley, E.E., 26, 101
Ripley, Edward, 77
Ripley, Frank, 77
Ripley, Lillie C. (Birdwell), 76
Ripley, Margaret, 71, 77
Ripley, Thomas, 71
Ripley, William H., 77, 77
Robertson, Annie, 77
Robertson, E.B. (Mrs.), 77
Robertson, E.R., 76
Robertson, Frank, 77
Robertson, J.W., 76
Robertson, Mary J., 77
Robinson, Cora F., 77
Robinson, John, 45
Rodger, 59
Rodgers, Delia, 78, 91
Rodgers, Ella D., 64
Rodgers, Evaleen, 80, 84
Rodgers, Evaleen Lady, 91, 101
Rodgers, Glenna, 64, 78, 91
Rodgers, H.F., 92
Rodgers, Henderson, 78
Rodgers, Henderson F., 82, 83
Rodgers, Henderson F. (Rev.), 64, 91
Rodgers, James D., 64, 80, 101
Rodgers, James D. (Jimmy), 82
Rodgers, James Dana, 91
Rodgers, Jimmy, 57, 83, 92
Rodgers, Laura, 64, 78, 91
Rodgers, Mae, 91
Rodgers, Mary, 64, 91
Rodgers, Mary Sue, 80, 82, 84, 91, 91
Rodgers, Mellie, 91
Rodgers, Robert, 80, 82, 83, 91
Rodgers, Robert F., 101
Roiston, C.A., 72
Roiston, Elizabeth, 71
Rose, Jeremiah, 71
Rothrock, 41
Rothrock, Mollie, 77
Rothrock, W.G., 77
Rothrock, Walter, 77
Rowe, Irene, 99
Rowe, John, 11
Rowe, Walter, 99
Rowles, 41
Rowles, Joe, 23
Royston, Russell, 24
Runyan, Bill, 11
Rupe, 42
Rupe, A.W., 64, 77
Rupe, A.W. (Mrs.), 77
Rupe, Bill, 15
Rupe, Ellie E., 64
Rupe, Mary A., 64

Rupe, Ruth, 42
Rupe, Tom, 42
Rupe, Will, 48, 77, 77
Russell, 20
Russell, Ann Steward, 53
Russell, Anna B., 64
Russell, J.R., 64
Russell, Jim, 4, 15, 53, 66, 70
Sampson, 41
Sampson, Harriett Melissa, 64
Sampson, Melissa, 13
Sampson, Ward, 13
Sampson, William Ward, 64
Scott, 41
Scott (Major), 45
Scott, Bill, 16
Scott, Charles, 11
Scott, Infant son, 64
Scott, Jessie, 77
Scott, John Gilliam, 64
Scott, John S., 23
Scott, Lydia E., 64
Scott, Lydia Ellis, 87
Scott, Major, 16
Scott, Mary, 77
Scott, Mary E. Conn, 64
Scott, Mehabe Ann, 71
Scott, Randolph, 9
Scott, Stellar, 77
Scott, William C., 64, 87
Scott, William C. (Major), 66
Sellars, Edjar, 77
Sexton, Dorothy, 80, 84
Sexton, Harlan, 81
Sexton, Harlin, 80
Sexton, Nancy, 84
Shields, 41
Shields, Joe, 9
Shields, Joseph, 71
Shoun, 4, 41, 80
Shoun, A.N., 8
Shoun, Clay, 73
Shoun, E. Clay, 64
Shoun, Eulalee, 35
Shoun, Eulalia, 77
Shoun, G.H., 8
Shoun, Ham, 15, 41, 53
Shoun, Infant, 64
Shoun, Lizzie T., 77
Shoun, Lizzie T. Morley, 64
Shoun, Roe, 28
Shoun, Roe D., 23, 64
Shoun, Theodocia Wilson, 8
Shoun, Tull, 28
Shoun, Tullie, 64
Shoun, Tullie M., 104
Simpson, James, 71
Skinnell, Joseph J., 77
Skinnell, Mary A., 77
Slagle, William G., 3
Slagle, William H., 97
Smith, Abraham, 67
Smith, Adelia, 77
Smith, Bill, 46
Smith, Cecil (Mrs.), 26
Smith, Davie, 42
Smith, Dicie L., 77
Smith, Frances, 77
Smith, Frank, 42
Smith, Henry, 77
Smith, Ina, 84
Smith, John, 79
Smith, John C., 26
Smith, Joyce Click, 14
Smith, Lucindia Moyer, 64
Smith, Pearle, 42
Smith, W.L., 77
Smith, William, 26, 67
Smith, William L., 64

Smythe, Clifford, 23
Smythe, Stanley, 23
Snapp, R.J., 9
Snapp, W.C., 9
Sneed, John, 71
Solomon, Mary Jo, 80
Southwood, Victor, 87
Spangler, Lidia, 77
Squibb, 5, 12, 24, 41
Squibb, Georgia R., 64
Squibb, J. Mell, 30
Squibb, Mel, 15
Squibb, Nellie O., 64
Squibb, Tommie, 64
Stanfield, Samuel, 67
Stanfield, William, 71
Stanton, Eppie, 84
Starr, James, 65
Stetson, John B., 17
Steward, Ann, 53
Stokes, John, 24
Stonecypher, Sammie, 24
Stoner, Deborah, 82
Stoner, Joseph, 82
Stoner, Patricia, 82
Stoner, Peggy Jean, 82
Stoner, Ralph, 82
Stphens, Emma, 77
Stphens, J.F., 77
Sullivan, Bill, 99
Sullivan, Chris Thomas, 99
Sullivan, Donald Joseph, 99
Sullivan, John Robert, 99
Sullivan, Martha, 99
Sullivan, Mary Thomas, 99
Sullivan, Patricia, 99
Sullivan, William Ted, 99
Swanay, Joe, 100
Swatzell, 24
Swiney, Ada M., 65
Swiney, Aldon, 65
Swiney, Beatrice, 65
Swiney, Hobert, 65
Swiney, James B., 65
Swiney, James I., 65
Swiney, L. Edgar, 65
Swiney, Minney E., 65
Syerly, John W., 65
Tame, Jim, 54
Taylor, Alfred, 6
Taylor, Butler, 70
Taylor, Nat G. (Rev.), 41
Testament, Marion, 15
Testerman, Cordia B., 65
Testerman, George, 65
Testerman, Hubert R., 65
Testerman, Patsy, 65
Thomas, 52, 59
Thomas, Buford, 25, 37, 42, 45, 48, 94
Thomas, David Reese, 16
Thomas, Duncan Reamer, 65
Thomas, Duncan Reesen, 65, 105
Thomas, Earle, 16, 24, 25, 66, 80
Thomas, Edith, 80
Thomas, George, 58
Thomas, Guy, 78
Thomas, Guy (Mrs.), 16, 24
Thomas, Guy Patton, 65
Thomas, Harry (Rev.), 11, 85, 86
Thomas, Harry E., 82
Thomas, Helen, 38, 99
Thomas, Helen M., 97
Thomas, Irene, 24
Thomas, J. Earl, 58
Thomas, Jack, 26, 101
Thomas, James Earl, 65, 78
Thomas, Jerry, 26, 101
Thomas, John (Dr.), 68
Thomas, Lulu, 16, 84

NAME INDEX

Thomas, Lulu (Mrs. Earl), 66
Thomas, Lulu White, 65, 82, 99
Thomas, Martha Baxter, 3, 25
Thomas, Mary Emily, 78
Thomas, Mattie Baxter, 105
Thomas, Mattie Baxter Reams, 65
Thomas, Newell, 80
Thomas, Niles Franklin (Jack), 65
Thomas, Norman, 58
Thomas, Reamer, 48
Thomas, Reece, 16, 24, 25
Thomas, Reese, 3, 34
Thomas, Sue, 94
Thomas, Sue Piper, 67, 74, 94
Thomas, Sue R., 33, 41, 49
Thomas, William Earle, 22, 65, 99
Thompson, 24
Thompson, Jennie, 77
Thompson, Sam, 43
Thompson, Samuel, 41
Thompson, W.P., 41
Thomson, Nathannel, 71
Tranbarger, Nova, 84
Tranbarger, W.D. (Rev.), 7
Treadway, James, 11
True, H.C., 74
Tucker (Dr.), 35
Tullock, David, 24
Turner, 99
Turner, W.H. (Rev.), 80, 85
Waddell, Andrew, 24
Waddell, Clyde, 14
Waddle, Samuel, 24
Walker, Clarence (Red), 45
Walker, J.M., 76
Wampler, George, 27, 94
Wampler, Terry, 94
Washington, George, 51
Washington (Gen.), 2
Watts, Kathleen, 82, 84
Watts, Michael, 82
Weems, 20
Weems, Bobby, 58
Weems, Mary E., 78
Weems, T.N., 77
Whinery, Joseph, 2
Whinnery, 42
Whinnery, B.F., 17
Whinnery, Joseph, 72
White, 42, 59
White, Alva, 42
White, Carl, 42, 78, 95
White, Charles B., 65
White, Charley, 95
White, Don (Rev.), 85
White, Earl, 3
White, Elbert Carl, 65
White, Elizabeth, 77
White, Elizabeth (Lizzie), 95
White, Elizabeth Ann Morley, 83
White, Elizabeth J. Morely, 65
White, Elizabeth Morley, 82
White, Elizabeth Morley White, 95
White, Elizabth Morley, 8
White, Elma, 65
White, Eula, 42, 43
White, Faye, 42, 43
White, Frank, 42
White, Franke, 74, 78, 83, 84, 95, 97, 99
White, Franke White Denney, 65
White, H.K., 23, 78
White, Henry, 9, 42, 78, 95
White, I.W., 65
White, Infant, 65
White, Infant son, 65
White, Infant twins, 65
White, Isaac, 8, 95
White, J.R., 23, 25, 74, 77, 99
White, Jack, 14, 22, 65

White, James, 82
White, James Henry, 65
White, James R., 9, 43, 52, 58, 67, 74, 95
White, James R. (Jimmy), 95
White, James Randolph, 65, 82, 96
White, Karl V., 65
White, Keene, 95
White, Lulu, 78, 95
White, Lulu Morley, 96
White, Mary E., 78
White, Mary Emily Good, 65, 96
White, Mary Good, 9, 25, 31, 74, 95
White, Mattie, 8, 95
White, Mattie V., 77
White, Minnie, 95
White, Minnie H., 78
White, Myrtle, 65, 75
White, Raymond (Rev.), 86
White, Walter, 65
White, Will, 78, 95
White, William Carl, 65
Whitwell, Dewey (Dr.), 85
Williams (Mrs.), 30
Williams, James, 78
Williams, James Hice, 78
Williamson, Clark, 41
Willis, Frank, 49
Wills, Ed, 80
Wills, Velva, 84
Wilson, 14, 41
Wilson, Amelia A., 65
Wilson, G. Randolph, 65
Wilson, Hardin, 65
Wilson, J.B., 31
Wilson, Joseph B., 16, 65
Wilson, Liza C., 78
Wilson, Margaret Ann, 65
Winslow, 59
Winslow, Addie, 65
Winslow, Fannie P., 65
Winslow, Gus H., 31
Winslow, James, 58, 59
Winslow, Mary M., 65
Winslow, Robert B., 65
Winslow, Ruth, 65
Winslow, Samuel B., 65
Winslow, Sarah, 65
Winslow, W. Clay, 64, 65
Winslow, Walter, 65
Wolfe, Mary, 84
Wolfe, Oscar, 11, 26, 101
Wolfe, Ralph, 11, 101
Wright, 42
Wright, J.C., 41
Wright, Jesse, 71
Wright, John, 2
Yakley, Martha, 65
Yakley, Mary E., 65
Yakley, W.H., 65
Yelton, James, 71
Yokley, 41
Yokley, Elsie, 42
Young, Annie L. Fisher, 65
Zimmerman, J.C., 78
Zimmerman, S.J., 78